CONFRON
WORLD GONE WRONG

CONFRONTING A WORLD GONE WRONG

8 sessions from Elijah's life on being God's person for God's purposes

M. Scott Miles

VICTOR BOOKS

A DIVISION OF SCRIPTURE PRESS PUBLICATIONS INC.
USA CANADA ENGLAND

Copyediting: Jane Vogel
Cover Design: Joe DeLeon
Cover Illustration: Richard McNeel
Interior Illustrations: Al Hering

Recommended Dewey Decimal Classification: 301.402
Suggested Subject Heading: SMALL GROUPS: 1 KINGS

Library of Congress Catalog Card Number: 92-2290
ISBN: 1-56476-023-5

1   2   3   4   5   6   7   8   9   10 Printing / Year   96   95   94   93   92

VICTOR BOOKS
A division of SP Publications, Inc.
        Wheaton, Illinois 60187

CONTENTS

PURPOSE: To help believers learn how to be God's person, in order to effectively live for God's purposes in a world that is difficult and secular.

INTRODUCTION

Confronting a World Gone Wrong is for people who want to learn how to be God's person, in order to effectively live for God's purposes in a world that is difficult and secular. An in-depth Leader's Guide is included at the back of the book with suggested time guidelines to help you structure your emphases. Each of the 8 sessions contains the following elements:

❏ **GroupSpeak**—quotes from group members that capsulize what the session is about.

❏ **Getting Acquainted**—activities or selected readings to help you begin thinking and sharing from your life and experiences about the subject of the session. Use only those options that seem appropriate for your group.

❏ **Gaining Insight**—questions and in-depth Bible study help you gain principles from Scripture for life-related application.

❏ **Growing By Doing**—an opportunity to practice the Truth learned in the Gaining Insight section.

❏ **Going The Second Mile**—a personal enrichment section for you to do on your own.

❏ **Growing As A Leader**—an additional section in the Leader's Guide for the development and assessment of leadership skills.

❏ **Pocket Principles**—brief guidelines inserted in the Leader's Guide to help the Group Leader learn small group leadership skills as needed.

❏ **Session Objectives**—goals listed in the Leader's Guide that describe what should happen in the group by the end of the session.

IS THIS YOUR FIRST SMALL GROUP?

'smol grüp: A limited number of individuals assembled together having some unifying relationship.

Kris'chən 'smol grüp: 4–12 persons who meet together on a regular basis, over a determined period of time, for the shared purpose of pursuing biblical truth. They seek to mature in Christ and become equipped to serve as His ministers in the world.

Picture Your First Small Group.

List some words that describe what you want your small group to look like.

What Kind Of Small Group Do You Have?
People form all kinds of groups based on gender, age, marital status, and so forth. There are advantages and disadvantages to each. Here are just a few:

❑ **Same Age Groups** will probably share similar needs and interests.

❏ **Intergenerational Groups** bring together people with different perspectives and life experiences.

❏ **Men's or Women's Groups** usually allow greater freedom in sharing and deal with more focused topics.

❏ **Singles or Married Groups** determine their relationship emphases based on the needs of a particular marital status.

❏ **Mixed Gender Groups (singles and/or couples)** stimulate interaction and broaden viewpoints while reflecting varied lifestyles.

However, the most important area of "alikeness" to consider when forming a group is an **agreed-on purpose.** Differences in purpose will sabotage your group and keep its members from bonding. If, for example, Mark wants to pray but not play while Jan's goal is to learn through playing, then Mark and Jan's group will probably not go anywhere. People need different groups at different times in their lives. Some groups will focus on sharing and accountability, some on work projects or service, and others on worship. *Your small group must be made up of persons who have similar goals.*

How Big Should Your Small Group Be?
The **fewest** people to include would be **4.** Accountability will be high, but absenteeism may become a problem.

The **most** to include would be **12.** But you will need to subdivide regularly into groups of 3 or 4 if you want people to feel cared for and to have time for sharing.

How Long Should You Meet?
8 Weeks gives you a start toward becoming a close community, but doesn't overburden busy schedules. Count on needing three or four weeks to develop a significant trust level. The smaller the group, the more quickly trust develops.

Weekly Meetings will establish bonding at a good pace and allow for accountability. The least you can meet and still be an effective group is once a month. If you choose the latter, work at individual contact among group members between meetings.

You will need **75 minutes** to accomplish a quality meeting. The larger the size, the more time it takes to become a healthy group. Serving refreshments will add 20–30 minutes, and singing and/or prayer time, another 20–30 minutes. Your time duration may be determined by the time of day you meet and by the amount of energy members bring to the group. Better to start small and ask for more time when it is needed because of growth.

What Will Your Group Do?

To be effective, each small group meeting should include:

1. **Sharing**—You need to share who you are and what is happening in your life. This serves as a basis for relationship building and becomes a springboard for searching out scriptural truth.

2. **Scripture**—There must always be biblical input from the Lord to teach, rebuke, correct, and train in right living. Such material serves to move your group in the direction of maturity in Christ and protects from pooled ignorance and distorted introspection.

3. **Truth in practice**—It is vital to provide opportunities for *doing* the Word of God. Experiencing this within the group insures greater likelihood that insights gained will be utilized in everyday living.

Other elements your group may wish to add to these three are: a time of **worship, specific prayer** for group members, **shared projects,** a time to **socialize** and enjoy **refreshments,** and **recreation.**

ONE

Getting Ready to Meet Our World

GroupSpeak: *"If I'm really living for God, then I won't have any choice—I'll always be in a state of confrontation with the world, won't I?"*

Learning to Live Our Convictions

Climbing a mountain takes know-how, the right equipment, and good physical conditioning. But more than these, it takes a certain kind of passion: a passion that drives you to reach for the summit regardless of the difficulty experienced on the way up.

God is looking for people who can pursue His purposes with the passion of a mountain climber. Elijah was one such person. Elijah's success was not in what he did, but in what he *was*. He was a man of conviction—conviction about God and God's relationship to His world. God is still looking for people like Elijah. Are you ready to climb the mountain?

GETTING ACQUAINTED

As I Understand It

Complete the multiple choice exercise below.

1. As I look at our world today, I feel . . .
   _____ scared _____ concerned

_____ excited _____ apathetic

2. Because of all the problems, I wish the world would...
   _____ go away and leave me alone
   _____ get right with God
   _____ explode into tiny pieces

3. Life in our world today is...
   _____ difficult _____ hopeful
   _____ unsure _____ easy
   _____ not worth the effort

4. If God called me to be a prophet, I would...
   _____ run and hide
   _____ have a long talk with God
   _____ pretend I didn't hear anything
   _____ answer enthusiastically
   _____ ask for another assignment

5. If I really were a prophet in today's world, I would...
   _____ tell people exactly what I think of them
   _____ launch a great evangelistic campaign
   _____ pray a lot
   _____ go quietly about my task
   _____ concentrate on changing one person at a time

If I Were God
What would you do if you had all the power of God at your disposal? Complete each sentence below.

❑ As I look down on our world, my first reaction is...

❑ Three things I would definitely change are...

❑ One thing I would not change is...

14

GAINING INSIGHT

Elijah's World — and Ours

Elijah's world was a tough place. Read 1 Kings 16:29-34. With a pencil, circle all the words or phrases that give clues as to the moral/spiritual condition of Israel, and of Ahab in particular.

²⁹In the thirty-eighth year of Asa king of Judah, Ahab son of Omri became king of Israel, and he reigned in Samaria over Israel twenty-two years. ³⁰Ahab son of Omri did more evil in the eyes of the LORD than any of those before him. ³¹He not only considered it trivial to commit the sins of Jeroboam son of Nebat, but he also married Jezebel daughter of Ethbaal, king of the Sidonians, and began to serve Baal and worship him. ³²He set up an altar for Baal in the temple of Baal that he built in Samaria. ³³Ahab also made an Asherah pole and did more to provoke the LORD, the God of Israel, to anger than did all the kings of Israel before him.

³⁴In Ahab's time, Hiel of Bethel rebuilt Jericho. He laid its foundations at the cost of his firstborn son Abiram, and he set up its gates at the cost of his youngest son Segub, in accordance with the word of the LORD spoken by Joshua son of Nun.

1 Kings 16:29-34

In the space below, write a brief character profile of Ahab.

How does this description parallel that of our own world today?

Elijah's Convictions — and Ours?

Elijah demonstrates three basic convictions necessary for the person God will use to accomplish His purposes in a difficult world. Read 1 Kings 17:1.

15

¹Now Elijah the Tishbite, from Tishbe in Gilead, said to Ahab, "As the LORD, the God of Israel, lives, whom I serve, there will be neither dew nor rain in the next few years except at my word."

1 Kings 17:1

Conviction 1: God Is Alive and in Control

Think of the many ways God reveals Himself today. Complete this sentence with as many responses as you can: "I know God is in control of His world because..."

God's sovereign control is very personal. Read the Scripture passages below.

¹³From heaven the LORD looks down and sees all mankind; ¹⁴from His dwelling place He watches all who live on earth—¹⁵He who forms the hearts of all, who considers everything they do.

Psalm 33:13-15

²¹Yet this I call to mind and therefore I have hope: ²²Because of the LORD's great love we are not consumed, for His compassions never fail. ²³They are new every morning; great is Your faithfulness. ²⁴I say to myself, "The LORD is my portion; therefore I will wait for Him."

Lamentations 3:21-24

²⁵"Therefore I tell you, do not worry about your life, what you will eat or drink; or about your body, what you will wear. Is not life more important than food, and the body more important than clothes? ²⁶Look at the birds of the air; they do not sow or reap or store away in barns, and yet your Heavenly Father feeds them. Are you not much more valuable than they?"

Matthew 6:25-26

Now circle three words from the list below that best describe how these verses make you feel.

dependent	accompanied	unthreatened
vulnerable	capable	overwhelmed
safe	upheld	peaceful
assured	empowered	nervous
confident	nurtured	loved
protected	aware	joyful

Conviction 2: Called and Set Apart to Serve God

Elijah appeared before Ahab because he knew God had called him and set him apart for a special and unique task. The Scriptures teach that every believer has been called to serve God in a special and unique way. To help you bring this into sharper focus, fill in the chart below. An example is given to get you started.

Living as One Set Apart	Not Living as One Set Apart
Spirit of seeking after God	Self-seeking and self-reliant

Conviction 3: God's Word Means What It Says

Elijah stood in the confidence that God's Word meant what it said. Do a brief Scripture search. Look up each passage below and record what it teaches you about God's Word.

❑ 1 Kings 8:56 _____

❑ Psalm 18:30 _____

❑ Isaiah 45:19 _____

❑ Luke 21:33 _____

❑ Romans 7:12 _____

❑ 1 Peter 1:23-25 _____

GROWING BY DOING

Confronting My Darkness
Isolate one area of your life in which you encounter the darkness of our world.

❑ The darkness I confront is . . .

❑ These three convictions can help me effectively confront this darkness by helping me . . .

Sharpening My Focus
List one way your life demonstrates each of these convictions:

#1: God is in control.

#2: I am called and set apart to serve God.

#3: God's Word means what it says.

Now list up to three specific actions you can take to grow deeper in how you express these convictions in your life.

GOING THE SECOND MILE

Going with God

Spend some time during the next few days thinking about your convictions. Then complete the following sentences.

❏ Because I know God is firmly in control of His world, one fear (or uncertainty) I can put to rest is ...

❏ Because I know God has called me to be His person in a special way, one task I can undertake for Him is ...

❏ Because I know God's Word is a sure foundation, my personal plan for getting to know His Word better is ...

Going with Each Other

Make a point of praying for our group as a whole this week. Find a prayer partner within the group to pray for specifically.

TWO

Coming to Terms with Our Expectations

GroupSpeak: *"I don't think it's unreasonable to expect God to take care of me. The big problem is knowing how to keep my expectations in balance."*

Realistic or Unrealistic?
What do you expect for rendering obedient service to God?

If we want to be champions for God's cause in His world, we need to sharpen our convictions. But we also need to come to terms with our expectations. God will often lead us into tough experiences that openly challenge our expectations of Him. Those experiences are seldom easy. Life is tough stuff, and God's champions need to be tougher.

God's person for God's purposes needs to learn to walk, live, and breathe in God's power. You can do that only when you learn to come to terms with what you expect from God because you serve Him.

 GETTING ACQUAINTED

Drawing the Bottom Line
Look at the set of lines below. On the top row of lines, write down five things you expect to receive from God in return for serving Him—one thing on each line. Then eliminate one of

21

those five expectations, and write the remaining four on the next row of lines. Continue this process until you have only one expectation left to write on the bottom line.

_____ _____ _____ _____ _____

_____ _____ _____ _____

_____ _____ _____

_____ _____

_____

It's My Right — Right?

Jot down some thoughts to this question: Do we have a right to expect anything in return for serving God? Why or why not?

GAINING INSIGHT

After delivering his message to Ahab, Elijah was thrust into a tough, difficult, grueling experience in the canyons of Kerith, the rugged desert wastes east of the Jordan River. Elijah would have to come to terms with three expectations through this experience.

Why Me? The Issue of Self

The "canyon experience" in Kerith exposed what Elijah may have expected for himself personally because he served God. Read 1 Kings 17:1-3.

¹Now Elijah the Tishbite, from Tishbe in Gilead, said to Ahab, "As the Lord, the God of Israel, lives, whom I serve, there will be neither dew nor rain in the next few years except at my word." ²Then the word of the Lord came to Elijah: ³"Leave here, turn eastward and hide in the Kerith Ravine, east of the Jordan."

1 Kings 17:1-3

22

In addition to saving Elijah's life, what possible reasons could God have for sending him into the canyon country of Kerith?

What kind of popularity did Elijah gain with his own people for taking a courageous and risky stand as God's champion? How was he viewed generally? How did Ahab view him specifically? (For some help, read 1 Kings 18:7-15.)

Put yourself in Elijah's place. You have just issued a challenge to an evil, powerful tyrant who actively opposes God. What would you expect to receive from God in return? Put an "X" on the lines below at the point where you would be between each set of extremes.

self-denial _____ applause
obscurity _____ recognition
hostility _____ public affirmation

Based on what you've learned about Elijah so far, where would you put him on the continuum above?

Have you ever felt that you should be recognized in some way for serving God obediently? Explain.

Why This? The Issue of Provision
Review 1 Kings 17:4-6.

⁴"You will drink from the brook, and I have ordered the ravens to feed you there." ⁵So he did what the LORD had told him. He went to the Kerith Ravine, east of the Jordan, and stayed there. ⁶The ravens brought him bread and meat in the morning and bread and meat in the evening, and he drank from the brook.

1 Kings 17:4-6

God could have easily provided more than such meager provisions, both in food and shelter. How would you respond to such arrangements if you were Elijah?

If you were God, how would you have provided for Elijah?

There were indeed other arrangements that would have been just as safe and much more comfortable (read 1 Kings 18:4). Why would God do less for Elijah?

Have you ever had an experience when you doubted that God could adequately provide for you? Have you ever had a time when God's provision seemed meager? Have you ever felt that God provided better for someone else than He has for you? Write about it in the space below.

Take a Survival Test. List below 10 things you value most to survive and live the way you feel is important (other than the essentials of life like food, water, oxygen).

1.	6.
2.	7.
3.	8.
4.	9.
5.	10.

Now, put a star (☆) next to those things you expect God to provide, a plus (+) next to those you expect to provide for yourself, and a zero (0) next to those things you expect someone else to provide.

How much do you really expect God to provide for you? Are your expectations realistic? Do you expect too little?

If God met all of your expectations and provided all you thought you deserved for serving Him, how would it impact your ability to live in God's power as His person?

Why Now? The Issue of Leading

A third expectation Elijah had to face was that of God's giving appropriate direction to his life. Read 1 Kings 17:7.

⁷Some time later the brook dried up because there had been no rain in the land.

1 Kings 17:7

Elijah had already suffered self-denial and meager provisions. Now he would suffer from the judgment on disobedient Israel that he himself pronounced! Why would God lead Elijah into a situation where he would experience this added difficulty of God's judgment on Israel?

God told Elijah he would be taken care of. While he would not enjoy a smorgasbord feast every day, he would at least eat regularly. Even meager provisions were better than nothing. What kind of questions do you suppose could have entered Elijah's mind after the brook dried up?

Think about it. You have followed God's leading. As a result you have landed in a situation that has gone from bad to worse. You wonder about God's ability to give your life adequate direction. In the space below, write down three feeling words that describe how you would feel in such a situation.

GROWING BY DOING

Coming to Terms

Think about what you expect from God *personally* because you serve Him. Consider what you expect God to *provide* for you because you serve Him. Reflect on how you expect God to *lead* in your life because you serve Him. Analyze your experience by completing the exercise below.

❑ A specific experience when I did what I knew God wanted me to do, even though it was a tough thing to do, or was completed at some personal risk was . . .

❑ A logical personal reward for such a personal act of obedience could have been . . .

❑ Things that God could have, or should have, provided for me as a result of this act of service were . . .

❑ Other options that would have been more desirable to me in that situation were . . .

❑ If God would have met all of these expectations, it would have affected my ability to grow as a person who lives by God's power by . . .

❑ By not meeting all of my expectations in this situation, I was better able to learn that . . .

❑ The most unrealistic expectation I had from God in this situation was . . .

❑ One specific way for me to come to terms with this expectation and put it to rest is . . .

GOING THE SECOND MILE

Going with God

Spend time during the next few days reviewing the exercise above. When you feel you have laid the specific expectation listed above to rest, then do the exercise again, substituting a different expectation of God that you feel you need to release in order to let God's power control your life.

Going with Each Other

Remember to keep praying for and supporting your prayer partner. Make an appointment to call him or her during the next week to encourage each other. Share together how you are doing at coming to terms with your expectations.

THREE

Refining Our Ability to Trust

GroupSpeak: *"God doesn't want me to let go of my things. He wants me to let go of me!"*

Putting Our Lives in God's Hands

Gold is refined by fire. As it is subjected to intense heat, all the waste, foreign matter, and anything else that would render the metal impure, is literally burned away. Nothing is left to dilute the worth of the metal. It is pure. The result is a metal of great value.

Life gets hot sometimes, doesn't it? And heat is seldom comfortable for any of us. Yet the heat we encounter in life serves a very important purpose in God's economy. It refines us. That is, it refines our ability to trust God—not just for the little things. Trust is not about easy believism. God uses the fire of life to help us trust Him for our very life. Becoming God's person for God's purposes means refining our ability to trust God fully for our lives. Elijah learned that kind of trust. And so can we. Let's turn up the heat!

 GETTING ACQUAINTED

Trust Is . . .
Think about what it means to fully trust God. Read the statements on the following page and circle your response.

29

Agree	Disagree	Fully trusting God means relying on His help when you find yourself in tough places.
Agree	Disagree	God wants us to be able to distinguish between the things we need His help with and the things we can handle with our own resources.
Agree	Disagree	In order to fully trust God we need to recklessly abandon everything in our lives to Him.
Agree	Disagree	Trust can take place only when we release God's power to work on our behalf.
Agree	Disagree	When we trust God we are able to allow Him to give us direction when He feels we need it.

How would you define *fully trusting God for your life?*

GAINING INSIGHT

Elijah exhibited three basic qualities of *full trust.* If we let God use life's heat to refine our ability to trust, Elijah's perspective can be ours as well.

Obedience Without Question

Elijah had just gone through a grueling experience in the canyons of Kerith. Now God asked him to do something that made no sense at all. Read 1 Kings 17:7-9.

⁷Some time later the brook dried up because there had been no rain in the land. ⁸Then the word of the LORD came to him: ⁹"Go at once to Zarephath of Sidon and stay there. I have commanded a widow in that place to supply you with food."

I Kings 17:7-9

Consider these reasons Elijah might have had for not going to Zarephath:

❑ He would have to walk across the hot desert wastes, in boiling temperatures, in a drought-stricken land.
❑ Zarephath was in Sidon, the homeland of Jezebel. He was going into enemy territory.
❑ Zarephath was the home of the god Baal, whom Elijah had defied with his prophecy. The people of Zarephath would not be real pleased to meet Elijah.
❑ Ahab had dispatched death squads into all the surrounding cities and countries. He would be going into a region where he could be easily spotted.
❑ Any widow in these times would have had little for herself to live on, let alone an additional houseguest.
❑ Jewish law forbade imposition on or taking advantage of a widow, both of which Elijah was about to do.

Put a check mark (√) next to the two reasons that would most make you question God's command to go to Zarephath.

List the factors or conditions that would make it difficult for you to obey a direct command of God that did not seem to make any logical sense.

What do you think is the relationship between full trust in God and obedience without question?

Faith Without Fear
Review 1 Kings 17:10-16. The strength and integrity of Elijah's trust continues to be apparent.

¹⁰So he went to Zarephath. When he came to the town gate, a widow was there gathering sticks. He called to her and asked, "Would you bring me a little water in a jar so I may have a drink?" ¹¹As she was going to get it, he called, "And bring me, please, a piece of bread."

31

¹²"As surely as the LORD your God lives," she replied, "I don't have any bread—only a handful of flour in a jar and a little oil in a jug. I am gathering a few sticks to take home and make a meal for myself and my son, that we may eat it—and die."

¹³Elijah said to her, "Don't be afraid. Go home and do as you have said. But first make a small cake of bread for me from what you have and bring it to me, and then make something for yourself and your son. ¹⁴For this is what the LORD, the God of Israel, says: 'The jar of flour will not be used up and the jug of oil will not run dry until the day the LORD gives rain on the land.' "

¹⁵She went away and did as Elijah had told her. So there was food every day for Elijah and for the woman and her family. ¹⁶For the jar of flour was not used up and the jug of oil did not run dry, in keeping with the word of the LORD spoken by Elijah.

1 Kings 17:10-16

Note the difference between Elijah and the widow. Fill in the chart below and compare.

	Widow	Elijah
Focus of trust		
View of the circumstances		
View of God		
Ability to act on trust		

Look at the following list. Rank each item as to the amount of fear it creates for you.

	LITTLE			MUCH
Losing your best friend	1	2 3	4	5
Not being able to pay the bills	1	2 3	4	5
Lack of job security	1	2 3	4	5
Loss of job	1	2 3	4	5
Losing your spouse and/or children	1	2 3	4	5
Having problems with your neighbor	1	2 3	4	5
Your house burning down	1	2 3	4	5
A tragic death in your family	1	2 3	4	5
Being a victim of violent crime	1	2 3	4	5
A crisis at church	1	2 3	4	5
Receiving obscene phone calls	1	2 3	4	5
Becoming emotionally unstable	1	2 3	4	5
Losing your physical health	1	2 3	4	5

Look at the fear you would rank highest. How can this fear stretch your trust in God?

Hope Without Despair

The heat in Elijah's life was suddenly turned up full blast, revealing the true worth of his ability to fully trust God. Read 1 Kings 17:17-24.

[17]"Some time later the son of the woman who owned the house became ill. He grew worse and worse, and finally stopped breathing. [18]She said to Elijah, "What do you have against me, man of God? Did you come to remind me of my sin and kill my son?"

[19]"Give me your son," Elijah replied. He took him from her arms, carried him to the upper room where he was staying, and laid him on his bed. [20]Then he cried out to the LORD, "O LORD my God, have You brought tragedy also upon this widow I am staying with, by causing her son to die?" [21]Then he stretched himself out on the boy three times and cried to the LORD, "O LORD my God, let this boy's life return to him!"

²²The LORD heard Elijah's cry, and the boy's life returned to him, and he lived. ²³Elijah picked up the child and carried him down from the room into the house. He gave him to his mother and said, "Look, your son is alive!"

²⁴Then the woman said to Elijah, "Now I know that you are a man of God and that the word of the LORD from your mouth is the truth."

1 Kings 17:17-24

God had been miraculously providing for Elijah and the widow's family for some time now. You would think that the widow would have become a bit more sensitive to the presence and power of God. Why do you suppose she reacted the way she did when her son died?

Elijah's composure stands in stark contrast to the woman's despair. She lived in the desperation of her circumstances. Elijah lived in the hope of the living God.

Does your trust demonstrate that same kind of hope? Read the four Hope Statements below. Check the one that best defines what hope is for you now.

❑ My hope is based on the assurance that God knows something about my life that I don't.
❑ My hope is based on the knowledge of where I am ultimately headed as God's child.
❑ My hope is based on the awareness that God is not a prisoner of my despair or my circumstances.
❑ My hope is based on the comfort that God is not finished yet, with me or with the world.

How is the hope statement you checked reflected in Elijah's response to the widow's despair?

34

Think of an experience in which this statement of hope really became meaningful for you. How did your hope affect your ability to fully trust God? Note it in the space below.

GROWING BY DOING

Unfinished Sentences
Read the unfinished sentences below. Write down one thing in response to each one. You may be dealing with a significant difficulty right now that would fit in all three sentences. Or you may have several different issues with which you are dealing that you can use to fill in the blanks. After you have completed all three sentences, choose the one you would feel most comfortable sharing with your small group.

❑ Something that makes it difficult for me to practice unquestioning obedience is . . .

❑ A fear that dilutes my faith in God's ability to care for me in the tough situations is . . .

❑ Circumstances I am dealing with that make it hard for me to be hopeful are . . .

GOING THE SECOND MILE

Going with God
As you read the following Scriptures, write down the specific point of strength that can be yours as you refine your ability to trust God.

¹⁰Many are the woes of the wicked, but the LORD's unfailing love surrounds the man who trusts in Him.

Psalm 32:10

Point of Strength:

³Trust in the LORD and do good; dwell in the land and enjoy safe pasture. ⁴Delight yourself in the LORD and He will give you the desires of your heart.

Psalm 37:3-4

Point of Strength:

⁵Commit your way to the LORD; trust in Him and He will do this: ⁶He will make your righteousness shine like the dawn, the justice of your cause like the noonday sun.

Psalm 37:5-6

Point of Strength:

¹Those who trust in the LORD are like Mount Zion, which cannot be shaken but endures forever.

Psalm 125:1

Point of Strength:

⁵Trust in the LORD with all your heart and lean not on your own understanding; ⁶in all your ways acknowledge Him, and He will make your paths straight.

Proverbs 3:5-6

Point of Strength:

²⁵Fear of man will prove to be a snare, but whoever trusts in the LORD is kept safe.

Proverbs 29:25

Point of Strength:

³You will keep in perfect peace him whose mind is steadfast, because he trusts in You. ⁴Trust in the LORD forever, for the LORD, the LORD, is the Rock eternal.

Isaiah 26:3-4

Point of Strength:

Going with Each Other
Continue to support your prayer partner this week.

FOUR

Confronting Our Counterfeit Gods

GroupSpeak: *"The real issue isn't, 'Do I have divided loyalties?' but, 'What do I do with the loyalties that are already divided?'"*

Who Do You Really Serve?

Remember the old western showdowns on television? The sun is blazing at high noon. Two men step into the street, facing each other. One is the town marshal. The other is the counterfeit—the one who wants to disrupt all sense of law and order and justice.

The duelers stand, each poised for the first strike. Suddenly, simultaneously, as if responding to a silent count, they draw. Shots ring out. Only the marshal is left standing. The counterfeit has been eliminated. Justice is restored.

Old West showdowns are not far from spiritual reality. Sometimes a counterfeit invades our spiritual life, competing for our attention. Spiritual loyalty can be compromised. Worship can be diluted. Devotion can wane. Elijah knew what a showdown was. He was the marshal that God appointed to challenge the spiritual counterfeits of His people. He was the one chosen to face Ahab and Israel with the truth of the living God. And he can help us face our own divided loyalties as well. So let's step into the street!

GETTING ACQUAINTED

Man's Best Friend

Look over the list of dogs below. Which one best describes the strength of your spiritual loyalties? Circle your answer.

Saint Bernard	Poodle	German Shepherd
Schnauzer	Golden Retriever	Siberian Husky
Basset Hound	Pekingese	Great Dane
English Bulldog	Chow	Bloodhound
Scottish Terrier	Pit Bull	Doberman Pinscher

List three favorable qualities about this dog that you feel characterize your spiritual loyalties.

On the Line

How would you characterize your devotion and loyalty to God? Look at the choices below. Place an "X" at the point where you see yourself between each pair of opposites.

Excited_____	_____Bored
Hot_____	_____Cold
Polished_____	_____Dull
Unbending_____	_____Compromising
Up_____	_____Down
Exact_____	_____Fuzzy
Radiant_____	_____Cloudy

Circle the word above that best describes the quality of your spiritual commitments. Why did you choose this word?

GAINING INSIGHT

After three years in hiding, Elijah emerges to face the spiritual disloyalty of Ahab and Israel. Through this intense encounter, three important lessons come through regarding the need to keep our spiritual loyalties strong.

Whose Fault? The Lesson of Consequences
Read 1 Kings 18:1-18.

¹After a long time, in the third year, the word of the LORD came to Elijah: "Go and present yourself to Ahab, and I will send rain on the land." ²So Elijah went to present himself to Ahab. Now the famine was severe in Samaria, ³and Ahab had summoned Obadiah, who was in charge of his palace. (Obadiah was a devout believer in the LORD. ⁴While Jezebel was killing off the LORD's prophets, Obadiah had taken a hundred prophets and hidden them in two caves, fifty in each, and had supplied them with food and water.) ⁵Ahab had said to Obadiah, "Go through the land to all the springs and valleys. Maybe we can find some grass to keep the horses and mules alive so we will not have to kill any of our animals." ⁶So they divided the land they were to cover, Ahab going in one direction and Obadiah in another.

⁷As Obadiah was walking along, Elijah met him. Obadiah recognized him, bowed down to the ground, and said, "Is it really you, my lord Elijah?"

⁸"Yes," he replied. "Go tell your master, 'Elijah is here.' "

⁹"What have I done wrong," asked Obadiah, "that you are handing your servant over to Ahab to be put to death? ¹⁰As surely as the LORD your God lives, there is not a nation or kingdom where my master has not sent someone to look for you. And whenever a nation or kingdom claimed you were not there, he made them swear they could not find you. ¹¹But now you tell me to go to my master and say, 'Elijah is here.' ¹²I don't know where the Spirit of the LORD may carry you when I leave you. If I go and tell Ahab and he doesn't find you, he will kill me. Yet I your servant have worshiped the LORD since my youth. ¹³Haven't you heard, my lord, what I did while Jezebel was killing the prophets of the LORD? I hid a hundred of the LORD's prophets in two caves, fifty in each, and supplied them with food and water. ¹⁴And now you tell me to go to my master and say, 'Elijah is here.' He will kill me!"

¹⁵Elijah said, "As the LORD Almighty lives, whom I serve, I will surely present myself to Ahab today."

¹⁶So Obadiah went to meet Ahab and told him, and Ahab went to meet Elijah. ¹⁷When he saw Elijah, he said to him, "Is that you, you troubler of Israel?"

¹⁸"I have not made trouble for Israel," Elijah replied. "But you and your father's family have. You have abandoned the LORD's commands and have followed the Baals."

1 Kings 18:1-18

Ahab roars onto the scene like an outlaw, guns blazing into the air, breathing threats and recriminations on Elijah. Why do you think he calls Elijah the "troubler of Israel"?

Elijah absorbed Ahab's blows and immediately turned the tables on him. Ahab was the one, along with his father's house, who had caused Israel's grief. What kind of trouble did Ahab create for Israel, and how did he do it?

Jesus had a great deal to say about the danger of losing grasp on our commitment to God. Read Matthew 6:19-24.

¹⁹"Do not store up for yourselves treasures on earth, where moth and rust destroy, and where thieves break in and steal. ²⁰But store up for yourselves treasures in heaven, where moths and rust do not destroy, and where thieves do not break in and steal. ²¹For where your treasure is, there your heart will be also.

²²"The eye is the lamp of the body. If your eyes are good, your whole body will be full of light. ²³But if your eyes are bad, your whole body will be full of darkness. If then the light within you is darkness, how great is that darkness!

²⁴"No one can serve two masters. Either he will hate the one and love the other, or he will be devoted to the one

and despise the other. You cannot serve both God and Money."

Matthew 6:19-24

Why are divided loyalties impossible?

What are the consequences of trying to serve two masters?

Any number of things can cause Christians to compromise their spiritual loyalties—pressures at work, financial strain, family stress, recreational pursuits. As you look at your own life, what kind of things could most easily direct your focus away from your primary spiritual commitments?

How Long? The Lesson of Choosing

Whatever you choose as your object of devotion is, after all, just that—your choice! That is what Elijah was about to teach Ahab and the people of Israel. Read 1 Kings 18:19-39.

19"Now summon the people from all over Israel to meet me on Mount Carmel. And bring the four hundred and fifty prophets of Baal and the four hundred prophets of Asherah, who eat at Jezebel's table."

20So Ahab sent word throughout all Israel and assembled the prophets on Mount Carmel. 21Elijah went before the people and said, "How long will you waver between two opinions? If the LORD is God, follow Him; but if Baal is God, follow him."

But the people said nothing.

22Then Elijah said to them, "I am the only one of the LORD's prophets left, but Baal has four hundred and fifty prophets. 23Get two bulls for us. Let them choose one for themselves,

43

and let them cut it into pieces and put it on the wood but not set fire to it. I will prepare the other bull and put it on the wood but not set fire to it. ²⁴Then you call on the name of your god, and I will call on the name of the LORD. The god who answers by fire—he is God."

Then all the people said, "What you say is good."

²⁵Elijah said to the prophets of Baal, "Choose one of the bulls and prepare it first, since there are so many of you. Call on the name of your god, but do not light the fire." ²⁶So they took the bull given them and prepared it.

Then they called on the name of Baal from morning till noon. "O Baal, answer us!" they shouted. But there was no response; no one answered. And they danced around the altar they had made.

²⁷At noon Elijah began to taunt them. "Shout louder!" he said. "Surely he is a god! Perhaps he is deep in thought, or busy, or traveling. Maybe he is sleeping and must be awakened." ²⁸So they shouted louder and slashed themselves with swords and spears, as was their custom, until their blood flowed. ²⁹Midday passed, and they continued their frantic prophesying until the time for the evening sacrifice. But there was no response, no one answered, no one paid attention.

³⁰Then Elijah said to all the people, "Come here to me." They came to him, and he repaired the altar of the LORD, which was in ruins. ³¹Elijah took twelve stones, one for each of the tribes descended from Jacob, to whom the word of the LORD had come, saying, "Your name shall be Israel." ³²With the stones he built an altar in the name of the LORD, and he dug a trench around it large enough to hold two seahs of seed. ³³He arranged the wood, cut the bull into pieces and laid it on the wood. Then he said to them, "Fill four large jars with water and pour it on the offering and on the wood."

³⁴"Do it again," he said, and they did it again.

"Do it a third time," he ordered, and they did it the third time. ³⁵The water ran down around the altar and even filled the trench.

³⁶At the time of sacrifice, the prophet Elijah stepped forward and prayed: "O Lord, God of Abraham, Isaac and Israel, let it be known today that You are God in Israel and that I am Your servant and have done all these things at Your command. ³⁷Answer me, O Lord, answer me, so these people will know that You, O Lord, are God, and that You are turning their hearts back again."

³⁸Then the fire of the Lord fell and burned up the sacrifice, the wood, the stones and the soil, and also licked up the water in the trench.

³⁹When all the people saw this, they fell prostrate and cried, "The Lord—He is God! The Lord—He is God!"

1 Kings 18:19-39

Note how Elijah set the stage for the showdown. Why would he want the false prophets, all 850 of them, to be there?

In the minds of Baal's prophets, Elijah had made a serious strategic error. Mount Carmel was Baal's home. If Baal could prove himself anywhere, it would be on Mount Carmel. Why, then, would Elijah choose this place for his contest?

What specifically was Elijah's challenge to Israel?

Take a look at the sad statement given at the conclusion of their ceremony in verse 29. What can this tell us about the problem of spiritual compromise?

Why did Elijah take such great pains to prepare the sacrifice?

What was God's ultimate purpose in confronting the apostacy of Ahab and Israel?

Like Israel, it can be hard for all of us to admit that we have been pursuing false gods with empty promises—especially when those pursuits seemed so innocent. In the space below, construct a Standard of Evaluation. List three questions you can ask yourself to determine if your spiritual loyalties are being divided by a particular pursuit.

☐ STANDARD #1: (example: Will it mean changing my spiritual priorities?)

☐ STANDARD #2: (example: Is this something that should occupy my mind?)

☐ STANDARD #3: (example: What does the Bible say about it?)

What's Left? The Lesson of Cleanup

God had revealed Himself in an awesome and terrible way. But the work was not yet complete. What would be done with Baal? Review 1 Kings 18:40.

⁴⁰Then Elijah commanded them, "Seize the prophets of Baal. Don't let anyone get away!" They seized them, and Elijah had them brought down to the Kishon Valley and slaughtered there.

1 Kings 18:40

46

After the fire fell, it was quite obvious that the empty promises of the false prophets had been silenced. Why, then, was it necessary for the people to put to death all of Baal's prophets? Could it have been handled in a different way?

Keeping our spiritual loyalties properly focused is a matter of putting our house in order. Read Psalm 127:1-2.

¹Unless the LORD builds the house, its builders labor in vain. Unless the LORD watches over the city, the watchmen stand guard in vain. ²In vain you rise early and stay up late, toiling for food to eat—for He grants sleep to those He loves.

Psalm 127:1-2

A door to God I would like to open is . . .

A window on the world I need to close is . . .

An area I would like to remodel is . . .

A place where I could use more insulation is . . .

A way to increase my curb appeal is . . .

Three words I would use to describe my house to a prospective buyer are . . .

GROWING BY DOING

Modern Psalms

Throughout the history of God's people, psalms and songs were commonly used to express adoration and commitment. Write a modern psalm of praise and commitment to the one real God that you serve. As your first line, use the words of the people of Israel in 1 Kings 18:39. "The Lord—He is God! The Lord—He is God!"

GOING THE SECOND MILE

Going with God

Read Luke 9:57-62. Reflect on what God is trying to teach you about the strength of your own spiritual loyalties. Then write a prayer of commitment to God in response.

⁵⁷As they were walking along the road, a man said to Him, "I will follow You wherever You go."

⁵⁸Jesus replied, "Foxes have holes and birds of the air have nests, but the Son of Man has no place to lay His head."

⁵⁹He said to another man, "Follow Me." But the man replied, "Lᴏʀᴅ, first let me go and bury my father."

⁶⁰Jesus said to him, "Let the dead bury their own dead, but you go and proclaim the kingdom of God."

⁶¹Still another said, "I will follow You, Lᴏʀᴅ; but first let me go back and say good-by to my family."

⁶²Jesus replied, "No one who puts his hand to the plow and looks back is fit for service in the kingdom of God."
Luke 9:57-62

Going with Each Other

What needs will you share with your prayer partner this week? How will you offer support?

48

FIVE

Building Our Prayer Relationship

GroupSpeak: *"I've been with people who make the hair on the back of your neck stand up when they pray! It's like you're all of a sudden on holy ground, or something. I've always wanted to pray like that."*

People Who Pray

Elijah was God's champion because he was a prayer warrior. After his victory on Mount Carmel against the prophets of Baal, he immediately went up on an isolated mountain peak to intercede with God on behalf of Israel. Would you have done the same? Let's go with him up the mountain and see what made his prayer relationship so strong.

GETTING ACQUAINTED

At the Movies

Complete the multiple choice exercise below.

1. The movie character that best describes the intensity of my prayer life is ...

____ Rambo   ____ Groucho Marx

____ Clark Kent   ____ Dirty Harry

____ G.I. Joe   ____ Mad Max

____ The Joker   ____ Indiana Jones

2. The movie title that best describes the consistency of my prayer life is ...

____ *Same Time Next Year* ____ *Monkey Business*
____ *No Holds Barred* ____ *Die Hard*
____ *Lethal Weapon* ____ *The Right Stuff*
____ *Home Alone* ____ *Predator*
____ *Bill and Ted's Excellent Adventure*

3. The movie theme that best describes the focus and content of my prayer life is ...

____ Disaster ____ Romance
____ Thriller ____ Adventure
____ Survival ____ Comedy

Analyzing Our Prayers
What do you pray for most? Analyze the content of your prayers. In the space below, list the things for which you pray most often.

Now try this. Look back over your list and evaluate.
√ Put a check mark by those items that are self-oriented.
☆ Put a star by those items that are family concerns.
+ Put a plus by the items that are needs of others.
– Put a minus by those items that are global or general in nature.

How much time during the week do you spend building your prayer relationship with God?

Based on the information you have recorded in this brief analysis, circle the two words below that you feel best describe the current status of your prayer relationship with God.

needy powerful weak

imaginative creative awful

growing	stagnant	flourishing
acceptable	active	anemic
borderline	stable	hurting

GAINING INSIGHT

As we look in on Elijah's prayer life, we'll observe three important things about his posture.

The Posture of Dependency
The contest was over. The people celebrated. But Elijah knew in his heart that God was not yet done speaking to His people that day. In Elijah's next move, we learn much about him as a man of God. Read 1 Kings 18:41-42.

⁴¹And Elijah said to Ahab, "Go, eat and drink, for there is the sound of a heavy rain." ⁴²So Ahab went off to eat and drink, but Elijah climbed to the top of Carmel, bent down to the ground and put his face between his knees.
1 Kings 18:41-42

What does Elijah's physical posture tell us about his spiritual posture as he prayed?

Elijah practiced complete dependency upon God in prayer. He did not presume to bask in the glow of the great victory won that day on Mount Carmel. Only God could bring the rain.

How would you define complete dependency in prayer?

What advances in our society encourage Christians not to exercise complete dependency and humility before God in prayer? Complete the sentence on the following page.

53

People today do not have to be dependent upon God because we have at our disposal . . .

How many of these things affect you personally? Put a star by the items that impinge on your ability to depend on God alone through prayer.

Choose one of the items you starred above. List three things you can do to practice dependency on God in your prayer relationship with regard to that item.

1.

2.

3.

The Posture of Expectancy
As Elijah stooped on Mount Carmel, head between his knees, he persisted in his confidence that God would answer his prayers. Read 1 Kings 18:43.

⁴³**"Go and look toward the sea," he told his servant. And he went up and looked.**

"There is nothing there," he said.

Seven times Elijah said, "Go back."

1 Kings 18:43

What doubts could have filled Elijah's mind?

Look at your own current life circumstances. What is the greatest, most needed thing you could expect God to do for you right now?

54

❑ My greatest life need right now is . . .

❑ Doubts or uncertainties restricting my ability to exercise total dependency and expectancy in prayer for that one need are . . .

❑ Ways I can release those doubts and uncertainties to increase my expectancy in prayer are . . .

The Posture of Focus

Elijah would not be deterred. He persisted until the completion of his petition was assured. Read 1 Kings 18:44-46.

⁴⁴"The seventh time the servant reported, "A cloud as small as a man's hand is rising from the sea."

So Elijah said, "Go and tell Ahab, 'Hitch up your chariot and go down before the rain stops you.' "

⁴⁵Meanwhile, the sky grew black with clouds, the wind rose, a heavy rain came on and Ahab rode off to Jezreel. ⁴⁶The power of the LORD came upon Elijah and, tucking his cloak into his belt, he ran ahead of Ahab all the way to Jezreel.

1 Kings 18:44-46

Review the entire incident (18:41-46). List the things that could have distracted Elijah from focusing on his prayer for rain.

List the things that might have the tendency to distract your thoughts and intentions when you pray.

Put a check mark (√) by one or two of these things that distract your focus the most. Then state one way you can eliminate this particular distraction.

GROWING BY DOING

Warriors of Prayer
There are many examples in the Bible of people who knew what Elijah knew about prayer.

❑ EZRA: So we fasted and petitioned our God about this, and He answered our prayers (Ezra 8:23).

❑ JOSHUA: "...As commander of the army of the LORD I have now come." Then Joshua fell face-down to the ground in reverence, and asked Him, "What message does my Lord have for His servant?" (Joshua 5:14)

❑ JEHOSHAPHAT: Jehoshaphat bowed with his face to the ground, and all the people of Judah and Jerusalem fell down in worship before the LORD (2 Chronicles 20:18).

❑ MOSES: "I lay prostrate before the LORD those forty days and forty nights because the LORD had said He would destroy you" (Deuteronomy 9:25).

❑ DANIEL: Now when Daniel learned that the decree had been published, he went home to his upstairs room where

56

the window opened toward Jerusalem. Three times a day he got down on his knees and prayed, giving thanks to his God, just as he had done before (Daniel 6:10).

How do the prayers of these individuals illustrate the postures of dependency, expectancy, and focus? Record your answers in the left-hand column of the chart on the following page. Then in the right-hand column, record how you can demonstrate those same qualities in your own prayer relationship.

HOW THEY DID IT	HOW I CAN DO IT

GOING THE SECOND MILE

Going with God
Take some time to sit down and plan a strategy to build your own prayer relationship with God. Use the statements below to lay out your plan. Then put your plan into action.

Place I will go to pray
Time of day that is best for me to pray
Length of time for me to pray
Excuses I need to stop using for not praying
What I need to do to prepare my "space" for prayer
Distractions I need to eliminate
Physical posture for most effective prayer for me
Aids and resources to help me pray more effectively

Going with Each Other
How can you encourage your prayer partner in his or her action plan? What support do you need for yourself?

SIX

Handling Our Down Times

GroupSpeak: *"I know life can really get you down. Looking at Elijah really helps me understand and cope better, rather than just sitting around and rotting in my own depression."*

So You're Having a Bad Day!

One minute you are riding the crest of the wave—hanging ten, having a thrill, experiencing the time of your life. Then, suddenly, you slip. You fall. You hit the bottom. And the wave comes crashing down on top of you. You feel like you are going to drown.

Being God's person for God's purposes does not insulate you from going through the down times of life. Some of your down times may be directly related to being God's person for His purposes.

After his showdown with the prophets of Baal, Elijah had a major down time. Let's see what we can learn from the way God responds to Elijah in the midst of his crisis.

GETTING ACQUAINTED

Ups and Downs

What have been the highest points in your life? What have been your lowest points? Label the Xs above and below the

59

line to chart the highs and lows of your life. Try to recall them in the order they happened. Then draw a line to connect the Xs, making it look like a graph.

X   X   X   X   X

   X   X   X   X   X

When I'm Really Down . . .
❑ When you are really down, what do you do?

❑ When I am having a bad day and need someone to talk to . . .

❑ When I need to do something to pick up my spirits, I . . .

❑ When I need to call someone on the spur of the moment to talk, I call . . .

❑ When I am facing a major crisis, my first response is . . .

❑ When I am in a major down time, my feelings about my self-worth are . . .

GAINING INSIGHT

Elijah's Crisis
Jezebel was fanatical about her religion. Elijah disrupted it by slaying all of her prophets. She began breathing murderous threats against him. So Elijah ran. He was afraid for his life. But why was he afraid? This was not the first time his life had been threatened. After all he had been through, why be afraid now? Quite simply, Elijah hit the wall.

Read the following verses from 1 Kings 19. Circle any key words or phrases that give you any clues to the nature of Elijah's situation.

60

¹Now Ahab told Jezebel everything Elijah had done and how he had killed all the prophets with the sword. ²So Jezebel sent a messenger to Elijah to say, "May the gods deal with me, be it ever so severely, if by this time tomorrow I do not make your life like that of one of them."

³Elijah was afraid and ran for his life. When he came to Beersheba in Judah, he left his servant there, ⁴while he himself went a day's journey into the desert. He came to a broom tree, sat down under it and prayed that he might die. "I have had enough, LORD," he said. "Take my life; I am no better than my ancestors." ⁵Then he lay down under the tree and fell asleep.

1 Kings 19:1-5

⁹ᵇAnd the word of the LORD came to him: "What are you doing here, Elijah?"

¹⁰He replied, "I have been very zealous for the LORD God Almighty. The Israelites have rejected Your covenant, broken down Your altars, and put Your prophets to death with the sword. I am the only one left, and now they are trying to kill me too."

1 Kings 19:9b-10

Elijah hit the bottom hard. If you didn't know better, it would be hard to believe this was the same person who raised someone from the dead, or who just called down fire from heaven. Note the symptoms of Elijah's depression. How and why did Elijah exhibit these symptoms? Fill in the following chart.

SYMPTOM	HOW?	WHY?
Feeling exposed and vulnerable		
Feeling loss of purpose		
Feeling depleted of energy		
Feeling futility, failure, isolation		

When you are in your down times, with which of these symptoms are you most likely to struggle? Why?

How do you generally handle it?

God's Prescription
God came to Elijah at specific points of need, and offered him healing. Let's look at God's prescription to Elijah's crisis.

First, God took the initiative to come and care for Elijah's personal need. Read 1 Kings 19:5-7.

⁵Then he lay down under the tree and fell asleep.

All at once an angel touched him and said, "Get up and eat." ⁶He looked around, and there by his head was a cake of bread baked over hot coals, and a jar of water. He ate and drank and then lay down again.

⁷The angel of the LORD came back a second time and touched him and said, "Get up and eat, for the journey is too much for you."

1 Kings 19:5-7

Though God took the initiative to provide for Elijah's specific need, Elijah had to willingly receive God's caring action. How about you? Is it easy or hard for you to accept God's care for you when you are battling the down times? Why?

God's care for Elijah was directed to Elijah's specific need for rest, food, and water. God's care for us in our down times is likewise suited for our own specific needs. What do you generally need most from God when you are down?

In what ways does He meet you at this point of need?

Second, God brought Elijah to a place where he could hear God's voice. Read 1 Kings 19:7-9, 11-13.

⁷The angel of the LORD came back a second time and touched him and said, "Get up and eat, for the journey is too much for you." ⁸So he got up and ate and drank. Strengthened by that food, he traveled forty days and forty nights until he reached Horeb, the mountain of God. ⁹There he went into a cave and spent the night.

1 Kings 19:7-9

63

¹¹The LORD said, "Go out and stand on the mountain in the presence of the LORD, for the LORD is about to pass by."

Then a great and powerful wind tore the mountains apart and shattered the rocks before the LORD, but the LORD was not in the wind. After the wind there was an earthquake, but the LORD was not in the earthquake. ¹²After the earthquake came a fire, but the LORD was not in the fire. And after the fire came a gentle whisper. ¹³When Elijah heard it, he pulled his cloak over his face and went out and stood at the mouth of the cave.

Then a voice said to him, "What are you doing here, Elijah?"

1 Kings 19:11-13

What was God's purpose in sending the wind, earthquake, and fire, before finally speaking in a gentle whisper?

List the ways God can choose to gently whisper to you when you are in a down time.

God has something special to say to each person in a major down time. It is personal. It is special. It comes in many ways and in many forms. The key for us is our own sensitivity to hearing God's voice. Think of the last major down time in your life. What do you think God might have been whispering to you in the midst of it?

Third, God refocused Elijah's purpose on the work that was yet to be done. Read 1 Kings 19:13-18.

¹³When Elijah heard it, he pulled his cloak over his face and went out and stood at the mouth of the cave.

64

Then a voice said to him, "What are you doing here, Elijah?"

¹⁴He replied, "I have been very zealous for the LORD God Almighty. The Israelites have rejected Your covenant, broken down Your altars, and put Your prophets to death with the sword. I am the only one left, and now they are trying to kill me too."

¹⁵The LORD said to him, "Go back the way you came, and go to the Desert of Damascus. When you get there, anoint Hazael king over Aram. ¹⁶Also, anoint Jehu son of Nimshi king over Israel, and anoint Elisha son of Shaphat from Abel Meholah to succeed you as prophet. ¹⁷Jehu will put to death any who escape the sword of Hazael, and Elisha will put to death any who escape the sword of Jehu. ¹⁸Yet I reserve seven thousand in Israel—all whose knees have not bowed down to Baal and all whose mouths have not kissed him."

1 Kings 19:13-18

Note what God told Elijah to do. List the people he was to contact and the part each would play in God's plan.

Note God's words of assurance about the 7,000 faithful people in Israel. What do you think God was trying to say to Elijah with this comment?

When we are in our own down times, it is easy to miss the bigger picture of all that God wants to do with our lives. One primary focus God has for all of us is to invest ourselves in the lives of others, just as He directed Elijah to do.

What particular task or ministry do you think God wants to refocus for you right now?

65

In whose life do you think God wants you to invest yourself right now?

What assurance can knowing these things give you when you are in the midst of a down time?

GROWING BY DOING

Can You Relate?
While you may not be able to perform the miracles Elijah performed, you no doubt can relate to the stress of his major down time. Think of something in your life right now that is creating a down time for you.

Check the symptom that is eating at you the most.

_____ feeling vulnerable, exposed, and unprotected
_____ feeling loss of purpose in my life
_____ feeling depleted of energy to go on
_____ feeling futility, failure, and isolation

Check the particular aspect of God's touch that would be most helpful to you in this situation.

_____ a caring action for a particular need I have in this situation
_____ gently whispering His wisdom in this situation
_____ refocusing the purpose of my life in His greater scheme

A Look at Our Downs
Think about those experiences that create a major down for you. Fill in the chart below to analyze them.

Experiences That Tend to Create a Down for Me	Symptom(s) Most Generally Present	The Aspect of God's Touch Most Helpful for This Situation

Complete this sentence:

As I look at the above information, one thing I can do to better handle my down times is . . .

GOING THE SECOND MILE

Going with God
Be alert to God's gentle whisper in your life this week.

Going with Each Other
Think of someone you know who is in a major down time. Write a note of encouragement reflecting what you have learned from your Bible study. Remember, this is a note of encouragement, not a sermon or a commentary!

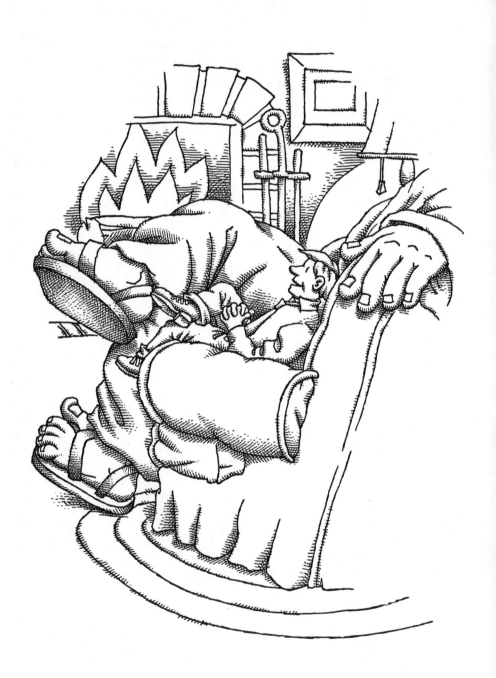

SEVEN

Learning to Live with Our God

GroupSpeak: *"I needed to hear this. I never really realized how easy it is to take God for granted."*

Do We Really Know Our God?
Learning to know who God is and what He is like is a requirement for anyone wanting to be God's person for God's purposes. Being God's person involves understanding God's nature and living in accordance with it. What is it that we need to know about God's nature in order to become His person for His purposes? Let's take a look!

 ## GETTING ACQUAINTED

Metaphors
How would you describe God? Complete each metaphor, illustrating what you think God is like.

❑ A SEASON OF THE YEAR that best describes God's character:

❑ A TIME OF DAY I am most aware of God's presence:

❑ A GAME that is most like my relationship with God:

❑ A WEATHER CONDITION describing the way God relates to me:

Picturing God ·
We can make a picture of God that consists of words, impressions, and characteristics. Let's try it.

His three most important attributes would be . . .

His main concern for the world would be . . .

The one thing that would make Him angry would be . . .

The one thing that would make Him cry would be . . .

The one thing that would make Him happy would be . . .

His perspective of my life would be . . .

GAINING INSIGHT

Ahab had died. His son Ahaziah had assumed leadership of Israel. Once again, God called on Elijah to confront a world in darkness. In this encounter between Ahaziah and Elijah, we can learn three very important lessons about the nature of God.

God Will Not Be Ignored
Read 2 Kings 1:1-8.

¹After Ahab's death, Moab rebelled against Israel. ²Now Ahaziah had fallen through the lattice of his upper room in Samaria and injured himself. So he sent messengers, saying to them, "Go and consult Baal-Zebub, the god of Ekron, to see if I will recover from this injury."

³But the angel of the LORD said to Elijah the Tishbite, "Go up and meet the messengers of the king of Samaria and ask them, 'Is it because there is no God in Israel that you are going off to consult Baal-Zebub, the god of Ekron?' ⁴Therefore this is what the LORD says: 'You will not leave the bed you are lying on. You will certainly die!' " So Elijah went.

70

⁵When the messengers returned to the king, he asked them, "Why have you come back?"

⁶"A man came to meet us," they replied. "And he said to us, 'Go back to the king who sent you and tell him, "This is what the LORD says: Is it because there is no God in Israel that you are sending men to consult Baal-Zebub, the God of Ekron? Therefore you will not leave the bed you are lying on. You will certainly die!" ' "

⁷The king asked them, "What kind of man was it who came to meet you and told you this?"

⁸They replied, "He was a man with a garment of hair and with a leather belt around his waist."

The king said, "That was Elijah the Tishbite."

2 Kings 1:1-8

Why do you suppose Ahaziah would seek help from Baal-Zebub, rather than from the God of Israel?

Based on Elijah's words to Ahaziah, how would you characterize Ahaziah's mistake in seeking comfort from Baal-Zebub?

How about it? Do Christians sometimes treat God as though He were irrelevant, unnecessary, and of little value? How so? Where is this tendency most likely to show itself?

God's message to Ahaziah was one of judgment. What are some positive reasons why God does not want to be ignored?

Do a Scripture Search. Note the ways God chooses to reveal Himself, and why it is not a very good idea to ignore Him.

¹O Lord, our Lord, how majestic is Your name in all the earth! You have set Your glory above the heavens. ²From the lips of children and infants You have ordained praise because of Your enemies, to silence the foe and the avenger. ³When I consider Your heavens, the work of Your fingers, the moon and the stars, which You have set in place, ⁴what is man that You are mindful of him, the son of man that You care for him?

Psalm 8:1-4

²Why do the nations say, "Where is their God?" ³Our God is in heaven; He does whatever pleases Him. ⁴But their idols are silver and gold, made by the hands of men. ⁵They have mouths, but cannot speak, eyes, but they cannot see; ⁶they have ears, but cannot hear, noses, but they cannot smell; ⁷they have hands, but cannot feel, feet, but they cannot walk; nor can they utter a sound with their throats. ⁸Those who make them will be like them, and so will all who trust in them.

Psalm 115:2-8

List some ways God chooses to reveal Himself.

List some reasons why it is not a good idea to ignore God.

God Will Not Be Bullied
Read 2 Kings 1:9-15.

⁹Then he sent to Elijah a captain with his company of fifty men. The captain went up to Elijah, who was sitting on the top of a hill, and said to him, "Man of God, the king says, 'Come down!' "

¹⁰Elijah answered the captain, "If I am a man of God, may fire come down from heaven and consume you and your

fifty men!" Then fire fell from heaven and consumed the captain and his men.

¹¹At this the king sent to Elijah another captain with his fifty men. The captain said to him, "Man of God, this is what the king says, 'Come down at once!' "

¹²"If I am a man of God," Elijah replied, "may fire come down from heaven and consume you and your fifty men!" Then the fire of God fell from heaven and consumed him and his fifty men.

¹³So the king sent a third captain with his fifty men. This third captain went up and fell on his knees before Elijah. "Man of God," he begged, "please have respect for my life and the lives of these fifty men, your servants! ¹⁴See, fire has fallen from heaven and consumed the first two captains and all their men. But now have respect for my life!"

¹⁵The angel of the LORD said to Elijah, "Go down with him; do not be afraid of him." So Elijah got up and went down with him to the king.

2 Kings 1:9-15

Some people never learn, do they? What lesson should Ahaziah have learned after fire fell on the first company of soldiers?

While few today would presume to try to use military force on God, many still believe that God is obligated to answer the demands of human decisions. They count God as a servant of their desires that they can use like a blank check.

Are there ways in which even Christians do this? Let's take a Perspective Test. Complete the following statements.

1. When I pray I . . .
   ❑ ask from God.
   ❑ seek after God.

73

2. When I serve God I . . .
   ❑ look for return.
   ❑ give with abandon.

3. When I worship I . . .
   ❑ focus on how it makes me feel.
   ❑ focus on praise and adoration.

4. When I use my talents I . . .
   ❑ focus on how well I perform my tasks.
   ❑ see it as an act of worship and stewardship.

5. When I review my monthly finances I . . .
   ❑ look primarily at the ending balance.
   ❑ have a great sense of dependence on God.

Review your answers. Can you isolate some specific ways that you tend to expect God to answer your bugle call, or count His power as insignificant to your life?

God will not be bullied or coerced by people like Ahaziah. Why does this truth make you personally grateful to God?

God Will Not Be Dishonored
Read 2 Kings 1:16-17.

¹⁶He told the king, "This is what the LORD says: Is it because there is no God in Israel for you to consult that you have sent messengers to consult Baal-Zebub, the god of Ekron? Because you have done this, you will never leave the bed you are lying on. You will certainly die!" ¹⁷So he died, according to the word of the LORD that Elijah had spoken.
                                                    2 Kings 1:16-17

How did Ahaziah dishonor God?

In what ways do people continue to dishonor God today?

What, then, does it mean to honor God?

If we dishonor God, as Ahaziah did, we cannot hope to live under His blessing. But when God's people honor Him, there is great hope.

Read Ephesians 1:11-14.

¹¹In Him we were also chosen, having been predestined according to the plan of Him who works out everything in conformity with the purpose of His will, ¹²in order that we, who were the first to hope in Christ, might be for the praise of His glory. ¹³And you also were included in Christ when you heard the Word of truth, the Gospel of your salvation. Having believed, you were marked in Him with a seal, the promised Holy Spirit, ¹⁴who is a deposit guaranteeing our inheritance until the redemption of those who are God's possession—to the praise of His glory.

Ephesians 1:11-14

List some words of hope and encouragement, from Ephesians 1:11-14, for those who want to honor God.

GROWING BY DOING

Making It Count
Isolate one area of your life where you can make specific applications of these three principles.

Now list one thing you can do to demonstrate each of these three principles in that area of your life.

❑ One way that I can demonstrate an awareness that God has a vital interest in all that happens in my life is . . .

❑ One way that I can demonstrate the realization that God's power and authority are all encompassing for my life is . . .

❑ One way that I can demonstrate a sense of the importance of honoring God in all that I do in my life is . . .

Evaluating Our Spiritual Relationship
As you review these three principles about the way God relates to you, which problem do you see most in your life?

_____ Ignoring God
_____ Bullying God
_____ Dishonoring God

List a few ways you feel you do this.

Now, list three specific actions you will take to improve in this area of your relationship with God.

1.

2.

3.

GOING THE SECOND MILE

Going with God
Spend some time this week reviewing the three actions you

listed above. In the space below, jot down a few additional things you could do to help you put your plan into action.

Going with Each Other
Enlist your prayer partner's support as you act on your plan.

EIGHT

Going Out in Style

GroupSpeak: *"Ushered out in a chariot of fire ... what a rush! If I can achieve only a small part of what Elijah did that qualified him for that kind of glory, then I'll be able to say I actually did something."*

Looking Good!

There is an old story about a rich man. It seems that when he died, he wanted to be buried in a gold Cadillac. So the mortician went to work and sculpted a great gold coffin resembling a Cadillac. At the funeral service, as this gold Cadillac was being lowered into the ground, someone in the audience was heard to say, "Man, ain't that livin'!"

Elijah is remembered as much for how he left the world as for what he did. Elijah went out in style because he lived in style. And in this last day of his life on earth, you can see a quality of life you can point to and say, "Man, that's livin'!"

Being God's person for God's purposes does not mean going out in style. It means living in style! We can learn much from Elijah about living in style.

GETTING ACQUAINTED

My Eulogy

What would you say at your own funeral if you could? Fill in the blanks below.

THE PERSONAL EULOGY OF _____

I, _____, left this earth

today as a result of _____ .

I am survived by _____ .

My chief goal has been _____ .

I hope my family will always be able to say of me that I

_____ . My friends and

coworkers will remember me _____

_____ . I will always be grateful

for the impact I was able to have in the lives of _____

_____ . The primary contributions I leave

behind are in the areas of _____ .

I always hoped that _____ .

I regret only that I was not able to _____

_____ . My last challenge and encouragement

to those I leave behind is _____ .

Epitaphs

In the space below, draw a gravestone. Then, write the epitaph as you would like it to appear on your stone.

GAINING INSIGHT

To what can we point and say Elijah lived in style? This passage will reveal several important observations about how Elijah lived in style, and how we can too.

Giving Encouragement and Challenge

Elijah somehow knew it was time to leave. Elisha also knew. He was determined to accompany Elijah to his point of departure—whatever that may involve. On Elisha's stubborn insistence, he accompanied Elijah on his last assignment. Read 2 Kings 2:1-5.

¹**When the LORD was about to take Elijah up to heaven in a whirlwind, Elijah and Elisha were on their way from Gilgal. ²Elijah said to Elisha, "Stay here; the LORD has sent me to Bethel."**

But Elisha said, "As surely as the LORD lives and as you live, I will not leave you." So they went down to Bethel.

³**The company of the prophets at Bethel came out to Elisha and asked, "Do you know that the LORD is going to take your master from you today?"**

"Yes, I know," Elisha replied, "but do not speak of it."

⁴**Then Elijah said to him, "Stay here, Elisha; the LORD has sent me to Jericho."**

And he replied, "As surely as the LORD lives and as you live, I will not leave you." So they went to Jericho.

⁵**The company of the prophets at Jericho went up to Elisha and asked him, "Do you know that the LORD is going to take your master from you today?" "Yes, I know," he replied, "but do not speak of it."**

2 Kings 2:1-5

God directed Elijah to visit two schools of prophets as his last act of ministry in the world. Why would God do this?

Think of all Elijah could say to these young men. What encouragement could he give them? What challenges might he lay before them? Jot some things down in the space below.

What qualities does a person have to possess in order to intentionally seek to build up and encourage others who are doing the work of God?

Do an "opportunity analysis." Answer the questions below.

1. Of those doing God's work, whom are you most likely to encourage and challenge? Check all that apply.

   ❑ pastor   ❑ Sunday School teacher
   ❑ close friend   ❑ neighbor
   ❑ church leader   ❑ spouse
   ❑ family member   ❑ other:

2. How do you most often do this? Check two.

   ❑ phone call   ❑ recognition award
   ❑ personal word   ❑ pat-on-the-back in passing
   ❑ written note   ❑ other:
   ❑ gift

3. How often do you do this? Check one.

   ❑ daily   ❑ twice monthly
   ❑ once per week   ❑ every few months
   ❑ more than once weekly   ❑ once per year
   ❑ once monthly   ❑ other:

How well do you do at encouraging and challenging those who faithfully serve God? How could you improve? Explain.

Release the Power of the Spirit
Read 2 Kings 2:6-10.

⁶Then Elijah said to him, "Stay here; the LORD has sent me to the Jordan."

And he replied, "As surely as the LORD lives and as you live, I will not leave you." So the two of them walked on.

⁷Fifty men of the company of the prophets went and stood at a distance, facing the place where Elijah and Elisha had stopped at the Jordan. ⁸Elijah took his cloak, rolled it up and struck the water with it. The water divided to the right and to the left, and the two of them crossed over on dry ground.

⁹When they had crossed, Elijah said to Elisha, "Tell me, what can I do for you before I am taken from you?"

"Let me inherit a double portion of your spirit," Elisha replied.

¹⁰"You have asked a difficult thing," Elijah said, "yet if you see me when I am taken from you, it will be yours—otherwise not."

2 Kings 2:6-10

Why do you suppose Elisha would ask for this particular gift?

What was Elijah's attitude and perspective on the issue?

By releasing the power of the Spirit in Elisha, Elijah was multiplying himself in a very real way. He had trained Elisha for ministry. Now he would not only release Elisha to assume his God-appointed role, he would release in Elisha the power of God's Spirit to carry out that role.

Is it easy or hard for you to release others to participate along side you in God's work? Circle the word (or words) that best describes the way you would feel in this kind of situation.

accepting	angry	open
partnership	refreshed	controlling
threatened	closed	participatory
involving	release	untrusting
stifled	insulted	rigid
willing	sharing	enthusiastic
begrudging	insecure	jealous
competitive	proud	encouraged
afraid	irritated	fulfilled

Reflect on the word (or words) you chose. What can you do to be more like Elijah on this point? Write it down below.

Carried by the Power and Presence of God
Read 2 Kings 2:11-14.

¹¹As they were walking along and talking together, suddenly a chariot of fire and horses of fire appeared and separated the two of them, and Elijah went up to heaven in a whirlwind. ¹²Elisha saw this and cried out, "My father! My father! The chariots and horsemen of Israel!" And Elisha saw him no more. Then he took hold of his own clothes and tore them apart.

¹³He picked up the cloak that had fallen from Elijah and went back and stood on the bank of the Jordan. ¹⁴Then he took the cloak that had fallen from him and struck the water with it. "Where now is the LORD, the God of Elijah?" he asked. When he struck the water, it divided to the right and to the left, and he crossed over.

2 Kings 2:11-14

Reflect on the phrase in verse 11, "As they were walking along and talking together." Project yourself into the situation. There was obviously a close connection between these two men. Elisha called Elijah, "father." He tore his clothes in grief at Elijah's departure. What kinds of things do you suppose Elijah and Elisha discussed as they walked along together?

When Elijah was swept away by the whirlwind, two things remained. His mantle fell to the ground; a continuing symbol and challenge for Elisha of his calling to ministry through Elijah. Elijah's footprints were also left, ending abruptly in the dust. Where Elijah's footprints ended, God's had begun. He was carried away by the power and presence of God.

Elijah left the world the way he lived in it—he was carried by the power and presence of God. He makes a statement several times in this passage illustrative of this fact, "... the LORD has sent me ..." (vv. 2, 4, 6). Think back on Elijah's life. How is the meaning of these words illustrative of the way Elijah lived his life with God? List some examples.

What would it take for you to be that totally committed to God? Take the Commitment I.Q. Test below.

1. If I could compare my Christian life to a football game, right now I am *(choose one)*:
   a. suiting up
   b. waiting in the locker room
   c. doing calisthenics
   d. in spring training
   e. sitting on the bench
   f. in the two-minute warning
   g. on injured reserve
   h. getting down and dirty
   i. _____

2. If I were to take this being carried in the power and presence of God seriously, I would have to *(circle one)*:
   a. change a few things about my life
   b. stop acting like a clown
   c. rearrange my priorities
   d. examine my value system
   e. take care of some hurting relationships
   f. release some hurt or bitter feelings
   g. _____

3. If I am going to be effective as God's person for God's purposes I will need *(circle two)*:

85

a. support from some close friends
b. a greater desire for God
c. a good kick in the seat of the pants
d. personal inner healing
e. all the help I can get
f. _____

Review your test and give yourself a grade. The extent to which you are being carried by the power and presence of God is *(check one)*:

A — excellent   D — poor
B — good   F — failing
C — fair

What is one thing you can do to bring up your grade?

GROWING BY DOING

Removing the Blocks
Think of the blocks that exist in your life that keep you from living in style, as Elijah did. How would you remove those blocks? Complete these sentences.

❑ A block that keeps me from encouraging and challenging others who faithfully do God's work is . . .

❑ A way to remove that block is . . .

❑ A block that keeps me from releasing the power of the Spirit in the life of someone else doing God's work is . . .

❑ A way to remove that block is . . .

❑ A block that keeps me from being carried by the power and presence of God is . . .

❏ A way to remove that block is . . .

GOING THE SECOND MILE

What can you do to live in style? Spend some time during the next week thinking about how to put the principles of this study into action. Complete the following exercise.

❏ I know I need to encourage others who are doing God's work because . . .

❏ One person I can encourage is . . .

❏ I know I need to release the power of God's Spirit in the lives of those who minister alongside me because . . .

❏ One person I can release is . . .

❏ I know I need to allow myself to be carried by the power and presence of God because . . .

❏ One way I can release myself is . . .

DEAR SMALL GROUP LEADER:

Picture Yourself As A Leader.

List some words that describe what would excite you or scare you as a leader of your small group.

A Leader Is Not . . .
- [ ] a person with all the answers.
- [ ] responsible for everyone having a good time.
- [ ] someone who does all the talking.
- [ ] likely to do everything perfectly.

A Leader Is . . .
- [ ] someone who encourages and enables group members to discover insights and build relationships.
- [ ] a person who helps others meet their goals, enabling the group to fulfill its purpose.
- [ ] a protector to keep members from being attacked or taken advantage of.
- [ ] the person who structures group time and plans ahead.
- [ ] the facilitator who stimulates relationships and participation by asking questions.
- [ ] an affirmer, encourager, challenger.

❏ enthusiastic about the small group, about God's Word, and about discovering and growing.

What Is Important To Small Group Members?
❏ A leader who cares about them.
❏ Building relationships with other members.
❏ Seeing themselves grow.
❏ Belonging and having a place in the group.
❏ Feeling safe while being challenged.
❏ Having their reasons for joining a group fulfilled.

What Do You Do . . .

If nobody talks—
❏ Wait—show the group members you expect them to answer.
❏ Rephrase a question—give them time to think.
❏ Divide into subgroups so all participate.

If somebody talks too much—
❏ Avoid eye contact with him or her.
❏ Sit beside the person next time. It will be harder for him or her to talk sitting by the leader.
❏ Suggest, "Let's hear from someone else."
❏ Interrupt with, "Great! Anybody else?"

If people don't know the Bible—
❏ Print out the passage in the same translation and hand it out to save time searching for a passage.
❏ Use the same Bible versions and give page numbers.
❏ Ask enablers to sit next to those who may need encouragement in sharing.
❏ Begin using this book to teach them how to study; affirm their efforts.

If you have a difficult individual—
❏ Take control to protect the group, but recognize that exploring differences can be a learning experience.
❏ Sit next to that person.
❏ To avoid getting sidetracked or to protect another group member, you may need to interrupt, saying, "Not all of us feel that way."
❏ Pray for that person before the group meeting.

ONE

Getting Ready to Meet Our World

Elijah stood as God's champion to confront the darkness of a needy world. Elijah is known as a prophet of power who performed great miracles on God's behalf. Yet Scripture calls him a man "just like us" (James 5:17). Elijah experienced life as we do—defeat, frustration, discouragement, hopelessness, depression, and severe circumstances. Even so, he emerged as a great prophet of power whom God used to confront the darkness of a difficult world.

God wants to make us into a people who can confront the need of a world gone wrong. What is the darkness of *our* world? What convictions are necessary to meet the challenge of a dark and difficult world? In this first study of Elijah's life, we can isolate both the need of our world and the convictions necessary to those God would use to confront this need.

As **Group Leader** of this small group experience, *you* have a choice as to which elements best fit your group, your style of leadership, and your purposes. After you examine the **Session Objectives,** select the activities under each heading with which to begin your community building.

SESSION OBJECTIVES

✓ To compare and contrast the condition of Elijah's world with that of our own.

✓ To define three faith convictions necessary to live effectively as God's person in today's world, as modeled by Elijah.

✓ To analyze and list specific actions each group member can take to build these convictions into the everyday expression of his or her faith.

✓ To establish prayer partnerships so that each group member feels the support and encouragement from at least one other member in the group on a continuing basis.

GETTING ACQUAINTED   20–25 minutes

Have a group member read aloud **Learning to Live Our Convictions.** Then choose one or more of the following activities to help create a comfortable, nonthreatening atmosphere.

As I Understand It

Read through one question at a time, state the options, and wait for each member to check an answer before proceeding to the next question. After you have finished, invite group members to share their responses and any additional comments to each question in turn.

Optional—Let's Make a Picture

Divide into smaller work groups of three to four people. Distribute a stack of newspapers and current event magazines, glue, scissors, and a piece of large construction paper to each group. Instruct work groups to clip headlines and pictures from their sources and glue them to the construction paper. The goal of each group is to make a collage describing the kind of world we live in. Allow about 10 minutes to work. Then have each group share its collage.

Ask, **What does it take to live effectively for God in today's world?** Many of their responses will no doubt be seen in Elijah's life.

92

If I Were God

Ask group members to share their responses to each question in the book. Note any similarities, inviting explanation or additional comment as necessary or appropriate.

Optional—Words, Words, Words

Divide into smaller work groups of three to four. Give each work group a paper and pencil. On a large sheet of newsprint list the following categories for the group to see:
- ❑ business and finance
- ❑ marriage and family
- ❑ school and education
- ❑ church and religion
- ❑ government and politics
- ❑ sexuality and morality

Assign each work group several categories. Instruct them to brainstorm up to five descriptive adjectives for today's world for each category assigned to them.

After 10 minutes, call time and ask for reports, recording responses on the newsprint sheet. Review all the words, then ask: **Based on this analysis of our world, what do you think God should do? Why?**

GAINING INSIGHT   30–35 minutes

Pocket Principle

1 Ask questions like, "Can you say more about that?" Or, "You've raised an important issue; can you help us understand where you're coming from?" Even simply asking, "What do you think?" or, "How do you feel about that?" can greatly assist group members in self-expression and self-disclosure.

Elijah's World—and Ours

A quick look at Israel's history helps us understand what was happening during Ahab's reign. During Solomon's reign the nation was prosperous and productive. But after Solomon died, rival kings rose up to assume power over the nation. Israel entered a period of civil war and apostasy. As a result, the nation divided—Israel to the north under Jeroboam, and Judah in the south under Rehoboam. Then came Ahab, the seventh of the northern kings.

Have the group read 1 Kings 16:29-34, paying particular attention to all it says about the state of Israel in general, and the character of Ahab in particular. Discuss their findings:

❑ **Write a brief character profile of King Ahab.** (Ahab was thoroughly evil, and plunged Israel into an unprecedented depth of spiritual and moral depravity. His marriage to Jezebel galvanized his morally twisted life. Jezebel was absolutely wicked, with an insatiable appetite for immorality and violence. Ahab and Jezebel both wallowed in a pit of utter depravity. There is no sadder statement to be made about any person or nation than the statement of 1 Kings 16:30, 33b. Israel teetered on the brink of extinction as the people of God. Time was running out fast.)

❑ **How does this description parallel that of our world today?** (It all sounds too familiar! Greed, violence, treachery, sexual immorality, all seem to be the norm in too many places in our world today. Reading this passage is like looking in a mirror. Our society is plunging headlong into a seemingly bottomless pit of depravity.)

Elijah's Convictions—and Ours?
Enter Elijah. Elijah bursts into the darkness of his time like a blazing torch. What do we know about Elijah? Actually, only what we read here. He was from Tishbe, of Gilead—a desert, mountainous region on the other side of the Jordan River. The people of that region were considered half-civilized shepherds and nomads who were steeped in desert survival. It's said they were more prone to fighting than talking. Elijah typifies all that is known of the people of that region—tough, rugged, abrupt, and intensely fierce.

When we read 1 Kings 17:1, we can isolate three basic convictions that recommended him to God for service at such a crucial time in Israel's history.

94

Conviction 1: God Is Alive and in Control

The prophetic message Elijah delivered was a direct challenge to Jezebel's god, Baal, the god of weather and agricultural fertility. Both Elijah's presence in the king's court and his message were a direct confrontation to Ahab's apostasy by the living and sovereign God.

Discuss these questions:

❑ **How does your relationship to the living God stand as a direct challenge to our world today?**

❑ **Through Elijah's prophecy, God was announcing to Israel that He still maintained sovereign control of His world. Is it easy or difficult for you to accept that picture of God today? Explain.**

❑ **What do you see in our world that threatens or supports your belief that God is alive and in control.**

❑ **How does it make you feel to think that God, in all of His power and sovereignty, can guide your life in very personal ways?**

Conviction 2: Called and Set Apart to Serve God

Ask your group members:

❑ **How would someone else know you consider yourself one who has been set apart to serve God? What characteristics would you exhibit?** (Direct the group's attention to the *chart listing* exercise in their books. Complete the exercise together, discussing each section as you complete it.)

❑ **Is such a conviction necessary for a Christian to live effectively in today's world?** (Many voices compete for our allegiances and loyalties today. Without a sense of calling to serve God we can only be driven like a reed in the wind. Our faith commitments will eventually be reduced to mere preferences among many other options.)

Conviction 3: God's Word Means What It Says

Elijah's message was a confirmation of a previous warning given through Moses in Deuteronomy 11:13-17. Read Deuteronomy 11:13-17, then discuss the following questions:

❑ **How does the fulfillment of Deuteronomy 11:16-17 apply to Israel under Ahab's reign?** (Israel had forsaken their relationship with God more under Ahab than any other king. God's warning to bring judgment on the entire nation must now come to pass. They had gone as far from God as they possibly could.)

❑ **What should this have told Ahab about the certainty of God's Word?** (When God speaks, Ahab should listen! The Word of God as given through Moses was known to Ahab, or should have been. Since he had forsaken the one true God to chase after false deities, Ahab would now learn that God meant what He said. If Israel was to be His people, they must then live according to His commands.)

❑ **How does placing ourselves on the authority of God's Word give us a place to stand in a world offering so many ways to achieve security and fulfillment?** (God's Word is the only unshakable foundation upon which we can build our lives, because God is a God who keeps His Word. He is faithful to His promises. In His love and mercy, He brings wholeness into the lives of those who walk obediently after Him. Nothing else in the world can offer that kind of assurance and security.)

Use the Scripture Search to see in what ways this witness of God's Word can give us courage to live in difficult times.

GROWING BY DOING   20–25 minutes

Confronting My Darkness
In groups of two or three, share how the convictions of Elijah can help you confront the darkness you encounter in your own life experiences. Covenant to pray for and encourage each other for the duration of the study course.

Optional—The Power of Conviction
Ask: **How have any or all of these convictions affected your life and relationships at home, at work, in your neighborhood, and at church? Do they influence the**

way you plan your activities, or the way you structure your priorities?

Then spend time thanking God for the opportunity to serve Him in His world, for His control in your life, and for His Word as a strength in which to live. Let your prayer thoughts be stimulated by your personal sharing.

Sharpening My Focus
Direct group members to complete the first part of the exercise as it appears in their books. As a large group, compile a list of specific ways these convictions are exhibited in the lives of persons in your group. Then pair off to complete the second part of the exercise.

GOING THE SECOND MILE   5 minutes

Challenge the group to spend some time during the next week thinking about how they can shore up these convictions in their own lives. They can complete the **Going the Second Mile** section on their own. Encourage group members to be praying for one another and help them choose prayer partners within the group.

GROWING AS A LEADER

One of the most important components of the success or failure of a small group is *accountability*. One of the best ways to achieve accountability is with a written covenant. Knowing what is expected sets a course for the group and frees members to channel their energies into group life. Specific items that can be included in a group covenant are beginning/dismissal time, specific group objectives, the balance of group activity (e.g., study, worship, prayer, etc.), child care, refreshments, absences, outside preparation, visitors, service projects, and the expectation for birthing a new group.

TWO

Coming to Terms with Our Expectations

Whatever else we may say about Elijah, of one thing we can be certain. Elijah was a man who learned how to tap into the source of spiritual power. But it was not something that came automatically. Simply having the right convictions about God was not enough to release that power in Elijah's life and ministry. This session will explore some of the other issues at stake, issues that were much more personal and intense.

As **Group Leader** of this small group experience, *you* have a choice as to which elements best fit your group, your style of leadership, and your purposes. After you examine the **Session Objectives,** select the activities under each heading with which to begin your community building.

SESSION OBJECTIVES

√ To identify the expectations of God each of us has because we serve Him.

√ To analyze ways we can lay our expectations to rest, in order to live more freely in God's power.

√ To reflect on and share personal experiences of inadequate or unrealistic expectations of God.

GETTING ACQUAINTED 20–25 minutes

Have a group member read aloud **Realistic or Unrealistic?** Then choose one or more of the following activities to help create a comfortable, nonthreatening atmosphere.

Drawing the Bottom Line
Individually complete the exercise. Then ask:

❑ **What criteria did you use to determine which expectations you could eliminate?**
❑ **Did the elimination process get easier or harder for you? Why?**
❑ **If this were the only expectation God would honor, how would it affect your service to Him?**

Optional—What Do You Really Expect?
Select four or five pictures from magazines depicting difficult situations or extreme conditions. Mount each picture on construction paper. Give each group member a 3" x 5" card. For each picture, ask the group: **What would you say to God or ask Him if you woke up tomorrow morning and found yourself in this situation?** Then ask: **What do our comments and questions reveal about what we expect from God?**

Optional—Disappointed
Give each group member a sheet of paper and ask them to write down a time when they were disappointed with God. Encourage them to be honest. It could be something major or minor. It may be something that happened to them, or something that happened to someone else that they know.

Next, direct them to write down three reasons why they were disappointed. After a few minutes, ask for volunteers to share their answers. Then ask: **What preconceived expectations of God are evident in our responses?**

Pocket Principle

1 When asking group members to share thoughts that are personal or that require self-disclosure, don't be afraid to allow

99

them the luxury of silent reflection. If the silence seems to go on too long without any sharing, perhaps your question has exceeded the ability of the group to disclose their personal thoughts. Or your question may be vague or confusing. As the leader, model the kind of sharing asked for by sharing your own answer first.

GAINING INSIGHT   30–35 minutes

Ask: **Do we have the right to expect anything from God in return for serving Him? Why or why not?** Entertain a few responses.

Why Me? The Issue of Self
Discuss the following questions:

☐ **In addition to saving Elijah's life, what possible reasons could God have for sending him into the canyon country of Kerith?** (There is more here than just saving Elijah's life. For Ahab, Elijah's disappearance was a symbolic statement that Elijah's message was indeed God's Word. The rain would only return at Elijah's command. If he was not there, no rain would come. But for Elijah, it was a matter of expectation. What did he expect to receive personally for obeying God at such great risk to himself? Certainly, a pat on the back, or a little recognition would be nice. But for Elijah, self-denial and obscurity were his rewards.)

☐ **What kind of popularity did Elijah gain by taking his courageous stand before Ahab?** (First Kings 18:7-15 gives clear indications regarding Elijah's popularity in Israel. He experienced hostility from his own people. He became known as the "troubler of Israel," rather than God's champion. Eventually, Ahab even dispatched death squads to look for Elijah.)

Work through the continuum exercise in the book. Invite group members to share their responses. Encourage open

100

sharing of their expectations. Work to clarify their responses when necessary and appropriate by asking probing questions.

Have group members look at the continuum again and mark where they think Elijah stood. Then ask: **Why do we sometimes feel we should be recognized in some way for our obedience to God?** (We are conditioned by our society to expect to receive something for services rendered. Further, all of us have a basic need to be recognized for what we do. We are also taught that God blesses those who serve Him faithfully. It's easy to desire applause or recognition when we serve God. We certainly wouldn't expect denial and humiliation.)

For us, the issue is one of what's fair for *me*, what personal benefit will there be for *me*. But for God, the issue is one of authority. It is a matter of who is in control. And on a personal level, it is a matter of who is in control of *you*.

Why This? The Issue of Provision
God told Elijah that He had made advance preparations for food and water. The ravens would bring him bread and meat twice a day, and he could drink water from the brook. While this sounds acceptable to us, to Elijah it might have seemed otherwise. The brook at Kerith was supplied by the runoff moistures from the higher mountain elevations. As the water trickled down, it gathered all the dirt and filth in its path.

As for the ravens, they were considered the garbage collectors of the desert. They scavenged food from the village garbage heaps, or from the rotting carcasses of dead animals in the desert. By Jewish law they were declared unclean.

Discuss the following questions:

❑ **How would you respond to such arrangements if you were Elijah?** (The issue of uncleanness of the ravens notwithstanding, Elijah probably had a question mark in his mind over the situation. At the least, God could have used a bird that was considered clean.)

❑ **If you were God, how would you have provided for Elijah? What other arrangements could He have**

101

made? (Generally, we tend to think God should provide for someone else the way we want Him to provide for us, don't we; especially in a case like this.)

❑ **According to 1 Kings 18:4, 100 prophets were lodged in a cave and ate food from the king's table. Why would God do less for Elijah?** (If Elijah could endure through the hardship of his severe circumstances and questionable provisions, then he would be able to face any challenge as God's champion. Being a person filled with God's power does not always mean having everything you need, or being comfortable and cozy. It may mean just the opposite. We need to learn not to doubt God can take care of us, even when all we have is bad meat and dirty water.)

❑ **Have you ever had an experience when you doubted God could adequately provide for you? Or have you ever had a time when God's provision seemed meager? Explain.** Help your group members bring this issue into focus through the Survival Test in their books.

❑ **If God provided all you thought you deserved for serving Him, how would it impact your growth as God's person who lives in God's power?** (People who get everything they think they deserve are usually self-centered, self-reliant, and self-absorbed.)

Why Now? The Issue of Leading

Elijah was God's champion. God took care of him. But even Elijah was not immune from the difficult period of drought that struck the land. He had already experienced self-denial and questionable provisions. Now he was led by God to a difficult place to experience the same judgment he had pronounced on an evil world. First Kings 17:7 says that Elijah's brook dried up.

Discuss the following questions:

❑ **Why would God lead Elijah to a place where he would suffer the same judgment he himself just pronounced on a disobedient Israel?** (Elijah needed to learn to follow God's leading no matter what it cost him personally. Just about the time Elijah might have thought

102

he had learned all that God wanted him to learn, the brook dried up. To Elijah, it might have seemed like a wasted experience. But to God, it was a matter of challenging Elijah's ability to trust His leadership.)

❑ **What kind of questions do you suppose Elijah might ask God about His overall judgment in this matter?** (God is the one who leads and we are the ones who follow. God is not in the business of staging a dramatic overkill to make His point. He is in the business of helping us come to terms with our expectations of His leading and care in our lives. And for that to happen the brook sometimes has to dry up.)

Encourage the group to complete the exercise in their books by listing three feeling words. Share and discuss what they have listed. Then ask: **What do your feeling words, and the discussion we just had, reveal about your expectations for God's leading in your life?**

GROWING BY DOING   20–25 minutes

Coming to Terms
Lead the group through the exercise in their books. Be sure to allow plenty of think time. Then encourage the group to share their experiences. Close your time of sharing by praying together regarding the specific points of application that were mentioned in the exercise.

Another option for prayer is to have everyone write down a specific point of application on a 3″ x 5″ card and trade with their prayer partner. Close in group prayer by having each one pray for the point of application written on the card.

Pocket Principle

2 Encourage your group to practice accountability in prayer. If group members request prayer for specific needs in their lives, be sure to ask them to bring a report back to your next meeting about

103

how God is working in that need. Group members will best learn to practice believing prayer on behalf of each other when they are able to see God working through their prayer efforts.

GOING THE SECOND MILE   5 minutes

Challenge the group to spend time during this next week working on the specific points of application they listed in the **Growing By Doing** section. Remind them to keep in touch with their prayer partners throughout the week.

GROWING AS A LEADER

Personal sharing and self-disclosure are important to small group dynamics. The level of sharing your group reaches will determine the extent to which your group bonds together and the depth of community you exhibit. But sharing does not automatically occur because we use a few "neat" sharing activities to stimulate interaction. Sharing is not an activity we do together. It is a process of revealing ourselves to one another. It takes more than a few well-planned sharing exercises to facilitate.

Evaluate how attentive you are as a leader to these influential factors:

❑ **Personal Expectations.** Does your group have a common understanding of how much each one is expected to share about himself/herself?

❑ **Relationships.** Do all the members of your group like each other? Are there personality clashes between certain individuals?

❑ **Previous Experiences.** Have certain group members had bad experiences in trying to share themselves in other settings, small group or otherwise?

❑ **Personal Investment.** Are your group members willing to invest themselves and share ownership in the process of group life?

❑ **Time.** How long has your group been together?

❑ **Leadership.** Does your style as a leader help facilitate or restrict personal sharing?

❑ **Threat Threshold.** Are group members expected to trust beyond what they are capable of at a given point in time?

❑ **Room Conditions.** Do the physical arrangements and condition of your meeting area encourage or inhibit sharing?

THREE

Refining Our Ability to Trust

The quiet confidence and assurance of one whose trust has been refined is attractive to those who are looking for a place to stand. How do we develop that kind of trust? We can learn from Elijah.

As **Group Leader** of this small group experience, *you* have a choice as to which elements best fit your group, your style of leadership, and your purposes. After you examine the **Session Objectives,** select the activities under each heading with which to begin your community building.

SESSION OBJECTIVES

√ To delineate the essential characteristics by which we demonstrate a full trust in God.
√ To define the kind of perspective needed to refine our ability to trust God.
√ To assist each other to trust God in a specific area of life and experience.

GETTING ACQUAINTED   20–25 minutes

Have a group member read aloud **Putting Our Lives in**

God's Hands. Then choose one of the following activities to help create a comfortable, nonthreatening atmosphere.

Pocket Principle

1 A natural tendency for discussion leaders is to want to offer commentary or interpretation on group members' comments. But the best sharing and group discussion take place when group members are responding to each other, rather than the leader serving as the go-between for group interaction. Group interaction is more meaningful to group members when they can help each other in the process of self-expression and interaction.

Trust Is . . .
Complete the exercise in the book as a group, reading one statement at a time, giving group members time to circle their response before moving to the next.

After adequate discussion time, divide group members into smaller work teams of two to three to write a definition of *fully trusting God* based on their discussion. Allow about five to eight minutes to work. Call time and share definitions.

Optional—Trust Walk
Divide your group into pairs and give each pair a blindfold. Have each pair do a trust walk—i.e., one person is blindfolded, and the other person leads him or her as they go for a walk. Do this outside if possible. After about five minutes or so, have partners exchange roles to repeat the process.

Afterward debrief by discussing the following questions:

❑ For what did you have to trust your partner during your walk?
❑ What were you feeling while you were being led on your walk?
❑ Was it easy or difficult to follow your guide? Explain.
❑ Was lack of control for your circumstance a problem for you? Why or why not?

❏ **How does this experience parallel what it means to trust God fully for all of your life?**

GAINING INSIGHT   30–35 minutes

If we want to be God's person for God's purposes, our trust needs to be refined so that we too can be people who trust God fully for our lives. There are three basic qualities of *full trust* that we can isolate from Elijah's experience.

Obedience Without Question
Ask: **If someone asked you to do something that made no sense at all would you:**
❏ **do it without question, complaint, stalling, or resistance?**
❏ **analyze the request and try to reason it out with the person making the request?**

Allow for a brief discussion. Then point out that this is exactly what happened to Elijah. God asked him to do something that made no sense at all, from a human perspective. But he did it anyway.

Read 1 Kings 17:7-9 and direct the group to complete the exercise in their books. Ask:

❏ **Of all these reasons, if you were Elijah, which two would be the most compelling for you to question God's command to go to Zarephath?** Give the group time to check their responses.

❏ **What are the factors or conditions that might make it difficult for you to obey without question?** (Answers may vary to this question. Several primary issues should surface. One revolves around what we ourselves may desire. If our desires conflict with God's, or if we are not personally comfortable with God's command, then our ability to trust God enough to obey will be hindered. Another issue is personal reward for doing something that does not make any sense. That is, why do something that is not the least bit reasonable if there is no obvious reward in it? Personal risk may also be a factor. In other words, what will happen if I do what God tells me to do? For others, it is a matter of wanting guarantees of a specific desired end result.)

❑ **What do you think is the relationship between full trust in God and obedience without question?** (If we are willing to trust God fully for our life, then we do not need reasons to obey. God is not looking for trained circus animals who need rewards, reasons, and physical motivations to jump through a hoop. He is looking for people who are willing to refine the quality of their inner character by fully trusting Him enough to obey without question.)

Faith Without Fear

Read 1 Kings 17:10-16 and lead your group through the chart exercise, comparing Elijah's perspective with that of the widow's. Point out that, from a human perspective, the woman's fear was not unwarranted. Given her circumstances, starvation was a very real problem. To feed Elijah would only accelerate the inevitable. But Elijah was not overwhelmed by the woman's fear. He knew what to expect of God, based on God's own promise. He could easily believe that God could provide for them both.

Lead the group through the ranking exercise in their books. Through your discussion, lead the group to understand that while all of us have some level of fear about certain areas of our lives, that does not negate God's ability to bring His power to bear on any situation that may come to pass. God has the ability to care for that which belongs to Him—and we definitely belong to Him!

Hope Without Despair

Direct the group's attention to the Hope Statements in their books. Have them check the statement that best defines hope for them now, and allow time for sharing experiences in which the statements of hope really became meaningful.

Ask: **Is there a circumstance in your life right now where you could use a little of this kind of hope?** Invite personal sharing only as group members are willing to do so.

109

GROWING BY DOING   20–25 minutes

Unfinished Sentences

Ask the group to reflect on the main points of the study by using the exercise in their books. After they have completed the exercise individually, divide them into teams of two, three, or four to share one of their answers. After each person shares, the others in the team should offer encouragement and supportive ideas for dealing with this area of trust.

Optional — Catching the Vision

Pass out several songbooks or hymnals and ask the group to turn to the song "Be Thou My Vision." Read the words together. Then ask the group to reflect on how the message of the song encourages them to apply the main points of the study and practice unquestioning obedience, faith without fear, and hope without despair.

Pocket Principle

2 Music is a great vehicle for assisting your group to worship God, and to express themselves to God in prayer. Take frequent opportunities to sing together. Singing before you begin your study can help focus the group on God's presence among you by His Spirit and through His Word. Singing during your prayer time can help you lift your hearts to God through the words that you sing.

Optional — Round Robin Sharing

Give each group member a piece of paper. Place a waste can in the middle of the room. Ask: **What one current experience or area are you engaged in where exercising Elijah's kind of trust is difficult for you right now?** Give a few quiet moments for them to think. Then let each one wad up his or her piece of paper, throw it in the waste can, and share that one thing. The act of throwing the paper in the waste can is symbolic of our desire to release ourselves fully to God's power to work in our lives.

GOING THE SECOND MILE   5 minutes

Challenge the group to spend some time during the next week thinking about how they can grow in their ability to trust God fully for their lives. They can complete the **Going the Second Mile** section on their own. Remind them to be in contact with their prayer partners during the week to encourage each other in their particular trust needs.

GROWING AS A LEADER

Bible learning that is most effective is that which is connected to life experiences. That is the way Jesus taught. He was able to capture people's attention and hold it for long periods of time. Why? Because He grounded His teaching in the life experiences of His hearers. To rural people He talked of sowing seed. To fishermen He spoke of the dragnet. To a Pharisee He taught on grace and forgiveness.

Your group is a rich resource of illustrations to apply the truth of God's Word. You will be most effective in leading your group in Bible study when you learn to find these points of connection. It will create a point of entrance for God's truth to touch their everyday world. This is Bible teaching at its best. And it can be done simply in these three ways.

❑ Use your own experiences to illustrate how a particular truth from God's Word has touched your own life experience. Be open and vulnerable. Don't just share your positive experiences. Share the hard ones, too.

❑ Use your group members' experiences to demonstrate how God's Word connects with them personally. Be careful, though, to be discerning in what and how you share. Know your group members well enough to know what they would not mind sharing with the group, and what they would rather keep to themselves.

❑ Use what has already been shared by your group members during the course of your time together. Referring to something shared earlier is a good nonthreatening way to help the group make personal connection with what they

111

study. It also affirms group members and encourages them to share more about how they are applying God's truth in their life experiences.

FOUR

Confronting Our Counterfeit Gods

So often our loyalties to God can be compromised. But when we place ourselves in the presence of God, His truth about our condition can blow right through us like a freezing wind. It cuts through our defenses, our smoke screens, and all the mental barriers we erect to protect our self-indulgences and self-interests. Without any question, God's truth quickly and completely exposes us for what we are.

First Kings 18 is the story about how the truth of an Almighty God cut through all the hardness of His people— much like a severe wind on a freezing cold day. Through it we can learn a few things about keeping our spiritual loyalties and devotion intact.

As **Group Leader** of this small group experience, *you* have a choice as to which elements best fit your group, your style of leadership, and your purposes. After you examine the **Session Objectives,** select the activities under each heading with which to begin your community building.

SESSION OBJECTIVES

✓ To isolate and examine areas in our personal lives
where we might nurture divided spiritual loyalties.
✓ To delineate the impact of nurturing divided spiritual loyalties on our growth as God's persons.
✓ To celebrate the reality of God as the one true God
through group worship and commitment.

GETTING ACQUAINTED   20–25 minutes

Man's Best Friend
Direct the group's attention to the exercise in their books.
When each one has shared, ask: **By which one of these
qualities of commitment would you most like to be
known by those who know you best? Why?** Divide the
group into small discussion teams of three or four to share
their responses.

On the Line
Lead the group through the exercise in their books. Then
divide them into discussion teams of three to four to share
their answers. After each group has shared their responses,
they should each choose and share the one word from the list
that best describes the strength of their spiritual commitment
now, and the one word that best describes what they would
like their spiritual commitment to be.

Optional—Taking Your Temperature
Give each group member a half-sheet of paper on which to
draw a thermometer that ranges from 0 degrees (at the bottom) to 100 degrees (at the top) with 10-degree increments
in between. Direct them to mark the degree setting that best
describes their spiritual temperature. Below that point, instruct them to list the positive factors that help them maintain that temperature. Above that point, ask them to list the
negative factors that keep their temperature from rising
above that point.

Let group members share their responses. Then ask: **Which**

114

one thing on this list is your number one hindrance to having a high spiritual temperature? Why?

GAINING INSIGHT   30–35 minutes
Pocket Principle

1 Often a group member will not ask a question for fear that it may sound silly or "dumb." In reality, the only silly or dumb question is the question that is not asked. Nurture an atmosphere of mutual respect which frees group members to ask whatever question that is on their minds.

Through Elijah's showdown with Baal's prophets, we can learn three very important lessons about self-examination and spiritual compromise.

Whose Fault? The Lesson of Consequences
Read 1 Kings 18:1-18. Ask the group to pay attention to the posture and attitude of both Ahab and Elijah. Ask:

❏ **Why did Ahab call Elijah the "troubler of Israel"?**
(Israel had suffered greatly through the drought. Livestock died. Some had to be killed. The drought caused a great famine as well. No doubt lives were lost as a result. If Elijah was the cause of the drought, his crime would be grievous. Ahab is like many in our world who stand and shake their fists at God rather than looking to the real source of their problems.)

❏ **What kind of trouble did Ahab create for Israel?**
(Ahab had only propagated the sin of his father in leading Israel down a path of complete moral and spiritual corruption. Ahab was always looking for an escape so he did not have to face the reality of the condition of his own heart. Elijah was an easy target.)

Read and discuss Matthew 6:19-24. As group members share their challenges, help them clarify what can happen to our devotion to God when other things become more important.

115

How Long? The Lesson of Choosing
Read 1 Kings 18:19-39 and ask:

❏ **Why would Elijah ask for all 850 prophets to be there?** (Elijah was called by God to confront the spiritual compromise of his world. If that compromise, and the consequences of that compromise, were to be exposed in the presence of God, then everything symbolizing Israel's condition needed to be there.)

❏ **Did Elijah make a strategic error in holding his contest on Mount Carmel?** (While in the people's minds Elijah would have made a serious strategic error, he was in fact a tactical genius! While everything about Carmel should have proved that Baal was alive and well, he was about to be proven to be a false god with empty promises. The one true living God was about to invade the lives of His people at the very point of their departure from Him.)

❏ **What can we learn from verse 29 regarding compromising our spiritual commitments?** (Whatever we allow to replace our devotion to God can never deliver on its promise. In fact, when these things are eventually placed next to the living God, they will prove to be little more than another Baal—a false god with empty promises.)

❏ **Why did Elijah take such great pains to prepare the sacrifice?** (When the time designated for prayer and worship in the Law had come, Elijah took over. He ordered twelve large jars of water to be poured on the altar and sacrifice. It could have been a symbol for cleansing. Water was used that way in the worship of God in the temple. It might have been for the salt. According to the Law, salt was to be used on burnt sacrifices as a sign of fellowship and covenant. Elijah's preparations were meticulous. If God's glory would be revealed to His people, everything must be just right.)

❏ **What was God's ultimate purpose in confronting Israel?** (Elijah's prayer indicates the real reason for the showdown. It was not to scare the people to death. It was to reveal the falsehood of their misdirected spiritual loyal-

116

ties, so they could be brought back to God. God made His point very clear. It was either Him or Baal—an all-or-nothing proposition. They could not have both.)

Divide the group into work-teams of three to four to construct a three-question "standard of evaluation." After five to eight minutes, call the group back together for reporting and discussion.

What's Left? The Lesson of Cleanup
Read 1 Kings 18:40. Ask:

❑ **Was it really necessary to kill all the prophets?** (Unfortunately, it would have been too great a risk to leave the false prophets around to continue to lead God's people astray. Judgment had to be exacted. Any other way would not have accomplished God's purposes.)

❑ **What can we learn from this?** (Sometimes it is hard to let go of those things that pull and play at our loyalties to God. But God's challenge through Elijah is quite clear. Are we willing to put away any last remaining remnants of the false gods that compete with our loyalties to God?)

Lead your group through the "spiritual house" exercise. The focus here is on strengthening personal devotion to God. Encourage group members to be as specific as they feel they can be.

Pocket Principle

2 Confidentiality needs to be given highest priority in a small group. Few things will erode sharing and dissolve trust like a small group member reporting personal information to others outside the group.

GROWING BY DOING   20–25 MINUTES

Modern Psalms
If it would add to the spirit of meditation and reflection, play some instrumental praise music as group members write

their psalms. After everyone is finished, stand up and form a circle. Go around the circle and have each one read his or her psalm. Join hands and ask group members to lead out in sentence prayers of praise and commitment.

Optional — Song Writing
Divide your group into teams of three or four. Hand out song books or hymnals with the hymn "My Jesus, I Love Thee." Ask each team to write a new verse for the song.

GOING THE SECOND MILE   5 minutes

Going with God
Challenge the group to spend some time during the next week thinking about how they can sharpen their spiritual loyalty and devotion to God.

Going with Each Other
Remind them to be in contact with their prayer partners during the week.

GROWING AS A LEADER

It is easy to sit down to prepare a group Bible study without first preparing ourselves. Even the most technically gifted Bible teachers will lack in their ability to illustrate personal identity with the application of God's Word if it is not a significant part of their lives. But preparing yourself to lead your group in study need not be a difficult task. Try one of these simple ideas:

❑ Read the Bible passage five or six times every morning between group meetings. Let God's Spirit call to mind specific points of application of the text for your own life. Try to make those points of application work for you during the day.

❑ Use your Bible study guide as a personal devotional guide. Do only a part of the Bible study each day. Focus on what you need to do that day to put into practice the specific application for which the Bible study calls.

118

❑ Take seriously the application exercises you will be asking your group members to put into practice. Work on doing what will be asked of them when you lead the study.

❑ Find a support person with whom you can meet regularly. Share with him or her what God is teaching you through the Bible study you are planning to lead.

FIVE

Building Our Prayer Relationship

Being God's person for God's purposes means cultivating a healthy relationship. Cultivating a healthy relationship with God requires building a strong prayer relationship with Him. It is through prayer that we meet with God face-to-face and express in words that which we feel inside. It is through that encounter that we hear God speak, and gain His direction and insight. It is through prayer that we maintain open communication with God.

James 5:17 says that Elijah was a man just like we are! When we see the power of his prayer, we might disagree. Yet, while we may not call down fire from heaven, we can tap into the secrets of Elijah's prayer relationship. We may not do what he did, but we can have that same strength.

As **Group Leader** of this small group experience, *you* have a choice as to which elements best fit your group, your style of leadership, and your purposes. After you examine the **Session Objectives,** select the activities under each heading with which to begin your community building.

SESSION OBJECTIVES

✓ To analyze several qualities of prayer necessary to build a healthy prayer relationship with God.

✓ To reflect on and discuss the habits and content of our prayer life.

✓ To engage in a directed experience of focused and supportive prayer.

GETTING ACQUAINTED   20–25 minutes

Pocket Principle

1 Leading a small group is a learned skill that takes practice to develop. No one does it perfectly all the time. And few do best on the first try. Learn from your mistakes, and let your ability grow as you grow together with your small group.

Have a group member read aloud **People Who Pray.** Then choose one of the following activities to help create a comfortable, nonthreatening atmosphere.

At the Movies
Lead the group through the exercise in their books. Then discuss: **What is the greatest need you have in your prayer relationship with God right now?** or **What is the greatest hindrance for you in building a stronger prayer relationship with God right now?**

Optional—The Ultimate Prayer Warrior
Divide the group into work teams of two, three, or four. Give each team a marker and a large piece of construction paper, and ask them to draw a humorous picture of what the Ultimate Prayer Warrior looks like. They should label and explain what each part of the warrior is for; e.g., ear plugs to block out distracting noises, knee pads for spending large amounts of time kneeling, etc.

Call time and have each group share their pictures. Then ask: **As you think about your own prayer relationship with**

121

God, which of these qualities just illustrated do you feel you do fairly well? Which quality do you think you could probably strengthen?

Analyzing Our Prayers

Lead the group through the exercise in their books. After you have finished the activities, divide the group into smaller discussion teams to share their responses as they choose.

Optional—Prayer Recipe

Divide into work teams of three or four. Ask each team to write a recipe, specifying the type and amount of each ingredient necessary for having an effective prayer relationship with God. Give five to eight minutes to work. Call time and ask each team to read its recipe.

Discuss these questions:

❏ **Which recipe fits your prayer life the best? Explain.**
❏ **Which recipe is least like your prayer life? Explain.**
❏ **Of the ingredients listed in these recipes, which ones are most active in your prayer life?**
❏ **Which single ingredient is your top strong point?**
❏ **Which is your number one weak point?**

GAINING INSIGHT   30–35 minutes

In these few short verses, we can observe a few key qualities that explain why Elijah's prayer relationship was so effective.

The Posture of Dependency

Read 1 Kings 18:41-42. Ask: **What does Elijah's physical posture say about his spiritual posture?** (Bowing low with your head down or lying facedown were typical postures of prayer in Elijah's day. They were symbolic not only of the seriousness of the petitioner, but also of his or her utter dependency before the Almighty God.)

Work in small work teams to define *dependency*. Dependency is based on the sensitivity to recognize who God is. God is the only one who can bring about that for which we pray.

122

Do the "sentence completion" exercise as a group; then ask group members to complete the second step and star those items that impose on their ability to depend on God alone through prayer. Divide into smaller discussion teams to share responses. Other group members in the team should suggest ways to practice greater dependency in their prayer relationships with regard to that item.

The Posture of Expectancy
Read 1 Kings 18:43. Ask the group to put themselves in Elijah's shoes and think of all the doubts and uncertainties upon which Elijah could have focused. Let them share these thoughts openly with the group.

Ask the group to consider their own life circumstances to pinpoint the things that impose on their ability to practice expectancy in their prayer relationship with God. Lead the group through the four statements in their books, allowing time for them to fill in the appropriate response after each one. Then ask each one to share his or her greatest need (if they are willing to do so), and one thing from each of the three remaining statements.

The Posture of Focus
Read 1 Kings 18:44-46 and list the things that could have distracted Elijah from focusing on his prayer for rain. (The noise from the feasting, the servant's presence or reports, and even the thrill of the victory could have distracted Elijah's focus. Even good things could have distracted him. He could have stayed to instruct Ahab, or spent his prayer time praising God for the miracle He had just done. He could have even spent some time praying for Ahab.)

 GROWING BY DOING   20–25 minutes

Warriors of Prayer
Together, read the Scripture passages about each character, and list the ways each one demonstrated any or all of the three postures that Elijah demonstrated—dependency, expectancy, focus. Then divide into smaller work teams to discuss how you can each demonstrate these same qualities in your own prayer relationship.

After ample time for discussion, instruct each work team to spend time lifting each other up in prayer.

Pocket Principle

2 **Because of the close relational proximity in a small group, you are encouraged to be personal—to discuss, to apply, to question, to seek. As you grow in obedience to God's Word individually, you also grow together as a group collectively. Your personal discipleship becomes an exciting pilgrimage within a caring, supportive fellowship of believers.**

Optional—The Practice of Prayer
Let your group experience the principles just studied by practicing them in a guided prayer time together. Choose one or two of the exercises in **Growing As a Leader** to lead your group.

GOING THE SECOND MILE   5 minutes

Challenge the group to spend time during the next week developing their own strategy for building their prayer relationship with God. Remind them to keep in touch with their prayer partners throughout the week.

GROWING AS A LEADER

Prayer is an important part of any small group experience. But there are many ways to pray other than simply going around the circle and praying for each request.

❑ **Conversational Prayer.** Let the group members make requests as they pray. Focus on that one item until it seems right to move to another need.
❑ **Directional Prayer.** As leader, mention one request at a time, along with a specifically desired focus for that prayer need. Pause to let the group pray silently for that item before going on to the next.
❑ **Circle Praying.** Ask each group member to state one

124

thing they believe God is telling them as a result of your Bible study. Then, go around the circle, having each person pray out loud for the person on his/her right (or left), specifically remembering the item mentioned.

❑ **Laying on Hands.** When someone shares a specific personal need, have the group gather around them to lay hands on them and pray for that need.

❑ **Prayer Wish.** When someone shares a particularly difficult life situation, go around the circle and have each group member offer him or her a specific prayer wish, completing the statement, "One thing I hope God will do for you is. . . ."

SIX

Handling Our Down Times

If we compared Elijah's spiritual experience with our own, we would probably conclude that Elijah lived far above our spiritual experience with God. He went through great tests and came out sterling. He performed great miracles on behalf of God. He is the epitome of spiritual power. That's why we need to see this side of Elijah, too. Though Elijah was God's champion, he was not superman. He too went through the pit of depression and despair. Let's look and see what we can learn from this one who has gone before us.

As **Group Leader** of this small group experience, *you* have a choice as to which elements best fit your group, your style of leadership, and your purposes. After you examine the **Session Objectives,** select the activities under each heading with which to begin your community building.

GETTING ACQUAINTED   20–25 minutes

Pocket Principle

1 **Time balance is essential for a good group meeting. Work with your group in establishing mutually agreed upon time breakdowns for each part of your group session: worship, study, prayer, etc. Write it down. Let the group review it occasionally to make any changes they feel would be helpful for group growth.**

Ups and Downs
Direct the group to complete the charting activity in their books. When completed, have each one share the high and low points in their lives.

When I'm Really Down ...
Have the group discuss the exercise in their books. Then ask: **What one thing makes the most difference to you when you are in a major down time?**

Optional—Walking Blind
Hand out blindfolds to all the group members. When they have each put their blindfolds on, ask them to stand up and spin themselves around three times. Then instruct them to find another seat on the opposite side of the circle and sit down. With their blindfolds still on, ask for one-word feeling descriptions of how it felt to be walking blind. Record their responses.

With blindfolds still on, ask the group to recall the most difficult experience they have faced in their lives. Again ask for one-word feeling descriptions of what these particular experiences were like. Record their responses.

Have them remove their blindfolds and return to their seats. Compare the two lists of words. Note the similarities. Indicate that the experience of walking blind is like that of any difficult time in our life.

GAINING INSIGHT   30–35 minutes

Anyone who wants to be God's person for God's purposes needs to learn from Elijah regarding handling the major down times of life.

Elijah's Crisis
Read 1 Kings 19:1-4, 9b-10 and work together to fill in the chart with the appropriate information. Use the following information to assist your discussion.

❑ **Exposed and Vulnerable.** As long as the drought continued, Elijah was relatively safe. Ahab knew he was the key to unlock the sky. Now rain had come. And there Elijah stood, within reach, exposed and vulnerable, with nothing to serve as a buffer between himself and Jezebel's fury.

❑ **Loss of Purpose.** Elijah's entire call had been wrapped up in prophesying the drought. Everything in his previous experience had prepared him for the showdown on Mount Carmel and the return of rain. He had carried out his mission. He no longer stood for anything. Confusion set in.

❑ **Depletion of Energy.** Elijah literally ran until he collapsed under a broom tree, totally exhausted. For three and one-half years he had lived on the edge of extreme intensity. He just ran over 100 miles. He had no physical or emotional energies left.

❑ **Futility, Failure, Isolation.** Elijah realized that in spite of the Mount Carmel exhibition, nothing had changed. Israel

128

still followed after false gods. Three and one-half years of waiting for that one day of triumph was wasted. It would all too soon be forgotten, and he along with it.

Lead the group to discuss the nature of their own down times. Let them share the symptoms with which they are most likely to struggle.

God's Prescription
Read 1 Kings 19:5-7 and discuss the questions listed.

Read 1 Kings 19:7-9, 11-13 and discuss the accompanying questions. Note that the noise of the natural forces stood in stark contrast to the whisper of God's voice. Elijah did not need to see God do a great sign. He needed to hear God's voice. For this to happen, God sharpened Elijah's senses by pounding the mountainside with the natural forces.

Read 1 Kings 19:13-18. This last part of God's prescription for Elijah is crucial. When we are in a major down time, we can lose all sense of perspective regarding our place in God's scheme. God has work for each of us to do. That work almost always will involve investing ourself in the life of someone else. Being God's person for God's purposes means making a difference in someone else's life for the sake of God's cause in this world. This is what God called Elijah to do next. Ask:

❑ **What did God want Elijah to do?** (He was to anoint Hazael king over Aram. Through him God would scourge and purge His people. Jehu was to be anointed king over Israel. Through Jehu God would judge all of Ahab's family. Elisha was to be anointed to succeed him as prophet. Elisha would become his servant, understudy, and close companion. Into Elisha, Elijah would pour himself for the rest of his days on earth.)

❑ **Why would God remind Elijah of the 7,000 faithful people in Israel?** (Elijah needed the assurance and comfort that comes from knowing that he was not alone. He was one of many whom God had chosen and called to be His people for His purposes.)

129

Lead the group through the personal exercise in their books. Then break them into discussion teams to share their responses with each other.

Pocket Principle

2 A small group can easily become in-grown if all its energies are focused only on the personal needs of group members. Work with your group to develop an outreach strategy or service and ministry projects to complete together.

GROWING BY DOING   20–25 minutes

Can You Relate?
Lead the group through the exercise in their books. Divide into small discussion groups to share their responses with each other. After each one shares, the other members of their team should offer one additional way they can plug God's prescription into their particular situation.

A Look at Our Downs
Have each group member complete the exercise in the book. Divide them into discussion teams to share and pray together in the manner described in the above activity.

GOING THE SECOND MILE   5 minutes

Challenge the group to spend time during the next week encouraging someone else who is going through a down time. Remind them to keep in touch with their prayer partners throughout the week.

GROWING AS A LEADER

Bible characters were real people with real feelings and real problems. By recalling our own feelings at particular points in our life experiences, we can more readily identify with a particular Bible character. Here are a few activities that can help you do this.

130

❑ **Remember the Feeling.** Determine the feeling, or particular response, on which your study focuses. Ask the group to remember a specific experience in which they felt that way.

❑ **Imaging.** Appoint a person to assume the role of the Bible character, and strike a stationary pose he or she believes demonstrates the emotions the Bible character is experiencing in the text—using facial expressions, physical posture, and contortions. Ask the group to give one-word statements they believe describe the feelings of the Bible character as exhibited by the group member.

❑ **Monologue.** Have group members write and read a monologue of the Bible character, reflecting the feelings of the character within the particular context of the Biblical passage you are studying.

SEVEN

Learning to Live with Our God

How much do we really know our God? Are we aware that He is always finding ways to invade our lives with His presence? We should be—that is, if we want to become God's persons for God's purposes. When we live in accordance with this simple principle, God can make us into persons like Elijah—His persons for His purposes.

As **Group Leader** of this small group experience, *you* have a choice as to which elements best fit your group, your style of leadership, and your purposes. After you examine the **Session Objectives,** select the activities under each heading with which to begin your community building.

SESSION OBJECTIVES

√ To analyze three principles by which God governs His relationships with His people.

√ To plan deliberate steps we can each take to learn more about how God relates to us.

√ To reflect on and discuss how we can each better respond to God on a daily basis, according to our understanding of how He relates to us.

GETTING ACQUAINTED 20–25 minutes

Pocket Principle

1 Often a group member's comments may leave a "loose string" that you can gently pull to assist him or her to further open his or her life to the group. Be attentive to these loose strings, and develop the art of using them to gain greater depths of sharing and personal discovery.

Metaphors

Complete the exercise in the book. Then divide into smaller discussion teams to share responses. After ample time for discussion, call the group back together and discuss:

❑ How much do you really know about God?
❑ What can you do to learn to better relate to God?
❑ In what one way would you like your relationship with God to grow?

Optional—Putting It on Paper

Supply the group with an assortment of various colored sheets of construction paper. Give them these instructions: (1) Select a color representative of your relationship with God, and (2) Tear out a shape that represents an aspect of God's character that is significant to you. After everyone is finished, lead the group to share their colors and shapes. Ask questions for clarification as necessary.

Picturing God

Complete the exercise in the book one statement at a time, having each group member share a response.

GAINING INSIGHT 30–35 minutes

As we examine Elijah's confrontation with Ahaziah, three very important truths emerge regarding how God relates to His world generally, and to His people specifically. When we live in accordance with those truths, we can indeed become God's persons for God's purposes.

133

God Will Not Be Ignored
Open your study with these questions:

❏ **What do you do when the phone rings and you do not want to answer it?**
❏ **Would it make any difference if you knew who was on the other end of the line?**
❏ **What if it were God on the other end—then what would you do?**

Probably all of us would answer the phone if we knew God was on the other end of the line. No one ought to ignore God! That was a lesson that Ahaziah had not learned yet.

Read 2 Kings 1:1-8 and discuss the following questions:

❏ **Why did Ahaziah seek help from Baal-Zebub rather than from the God of Israel?** (The apple does not fall far from the tree, does it? Ahaziah was just like his father in religious perversion. Like his father, he preferred a counterfeit—a false god with empty promises.)

❏ **According to Elijah's words, what was Ahaziah's mistake?** (Like his father before him, Ahaziah assumed that God did not really matter as long as there was a reasonable substitute. As long as he could find help in other places, he believed God was irrelevant and unnecessary.)

As you complete and discuss the rest of the exercises in this section, note that out of God's great love and grace, He desires to be involved in our lives in a very personal way. Therefore, He takes the initiative to invade our lives with His presence so we can be touched by His mercy.

God Will Not Be Bullied
Read 2 Kings 1:9-15. Note the attempt of the soldiers to take Elijah by force. He should have learned after the first time that God cannot be bullied, coerced, or otherwise beaten into submission by any person.

Lead the group through the Perspective Test in their books. Discuss what group members might have learned about

134

themselves by reflecting on their answers. We can sometimes be infatuated with our own strength, skills, or self-
worth. But God has not put us on earth to simply adminis-
trate things in His absence. God does not answer anyone's
bugle call. Our choices do not determine His commitments.
His decisions are not based on our value judgments; neither
are they influenced by our opinions.

With people like Ahaziah around, this great truth should give
us great comfort. Think of how the world would be if God
took orders from any one human being! That is why we
cannot bully or coerce God.

God Will Not Be Dishonored

Read 2 Kings 1:16-18 and discuss the following questions:

❏ **In what ways did Ahaziah dishonor God?** (This whole
incident is illustrative of Ahaziah's inability to honor God.
He wrongly assumed God counted for nothing. In his arrogance he attempted to take God by force. And he sought
assistance from a counterfeit god, rather than from the one
true God. The hardness of Ahaziah's heart toward God is
finally revealed when, after Elijah's message of judgment,
Ahaziah demonstrated no tendency toward repentance. He
died in his arrogance.)

❏ **In what ways do people continue today to dishonor
God?** (Like Ahaziah, our contemporary world is arrogant
and self-centered. Man's opinion is the only one that
counts. God is unimportant. Man's dishonor of God happens today as it did for Ahaziah. He is neglected, ignored,
bullied, belittled, and cursed.)

❏ **What does it mean to honor God?** (Refer the group to
Deuteronomy 11:13-17. Note that these verses were re-
viewed in the first session of this study. God indicated to
Israel that honoring Him meant that they were to love,
serve, and obey Him only. Viewed this way, the concept of
honoring God is really quite simple.)

As you work through the Ephesians 1:11-14 listing exercise
in the book, recognize that God created us for His honor and

glory. Through the work of Christ in our lives, we have all we need to serve the purposes of God in our lives.

GROWING BY DOING   20–25 minutes

Making It Count
Complete the exercise in the book, then divide into discussion teams of three or four to share responses to the exercise. Each one should state one way the others in their team can specifically pray for them in relation to what they have shared. Each team can then spend the balance of their time praying for one another.

Evaluating Our Spiritual Relationship
Complete the exercise in the book and the process in the previous activity for a sharing and concluding prayer activity.

GOING THE SECOND MILE   5 minutes

Challenge the group to spend time during the next week learning to know God better by working through the plan they each developed in the **Growing By Doing** section. Remind them to keep in touch with their prayer partners.

GROWING AS A LEADER

Every small group moves through four stages in its life together. You can easily remember them when you think in terms of Jell-O!

❑ **The Mixing Stage** is the warmth and thrill of getting started. Your role as leader is to facilitate the getting acquainted process, set an example of openness and acceptance, provide a comfortable setting, keep things simple, and focus on sharing personal histories.

❑ **The Gelling Stage** is when the elements settle and begin feeling a sense of discomfort as expectations are solidified and threat levels emerge. Your role as leader is to guide the group by clarifying expectations, facilitating conflict

136

resolution, being an encourager, working at group communication, keeping the group on target with its objectives, showing sensitivity to trust-threat levels, and using the Bible study as a common ground for sharing.

❏ **The Cohesion Stage** is when all the elements have molded together into a solid supportive unit. Your role as leader is to emphasize support, encourage and affirm the group process, channel the high relational energy into service and outreach, and work on preparing the group for adding new members or birthing a new group.

❏ **The Rubber-Izing Stage** is when a feeling of final maintenance level is reached. Your role as leader is to assist the group members to affirm the values of their group experience and begin preparing the group for termination.

EIGHT

Going Out in Style

Most of us have visions of going out of the world in a blaze of glory, or with some great achievement attached to our name. But in reality our notoriety will not be in how we are buried, but in what we did with our lives. Elijah left this earth in a blaze of glory, literally! But his going was symbolic of his living. He went in style because he lived in style. Want to be God's person for God's purposes? Then live in style!

As **Group Leader** of this small group experience, *you* have a choice as to which elements best fit your group, your style of leadership, and your purposes. After you examine the **Session Objectives,** select the activities under each heading with which to begin your community building.

SESSION OBJECTIVES

√ To name and illustrate things for which we would like to be remembered at the end of our lives.

√ To discuss the important qualities necessary for having an impact for God in our world.

√ To rejoice over the privilege to be God's person for God's purposes.

√ To design a plan to live an attractive life that will impact the lives of others.

138

GETTING ACQUAINTED 20–25 minutes

Have a group member read aloud **Looking Good!** Then choose one or more of the following activities to help create a comfortable, nonthreatening atmosphere.

My Eulogy
Complete the exercise in the book, then discuss what each member has written.

Epitaphs
Divide into small discussion teams of three or four and let group members share their epitaphs with each other.

Optional—"You're OK, I'm . . ."
Hand out a blank piece of paper to each group member. Instruct them to draw a line down the middle. At the top of the left column they should each write the word "Me." At the top of the right column, they should write the word "You." Direct them to write five positive descriptive statements about themselves in the left column, focusing on *qualities* rather than *roles*.

Divide into pairs. Ask them to write five statements in the second column describing positive qualities they see in their partner. Each pair should share their responses with each other, noting similarities and differences on the two lists. Call the group back together and discuss:

❑ How different/similar was your own list from how your partner sees you?
❑ Which list did you like better? Why?
❑ Choose one quality from each list by which you would like to be remembered most after you leave this world. Why did you choose those two qualities?

Pocket Principle

1 Try beginning your small group sessions with an opportunity for group members to report an experience of how they applied the principles from the Bible study of the previous session.

139

GAINING INSIGHT   30–35 minutes

Before looking at the Bible text, ask your group to consider:

❑ **How would you spend your last day on earth if you were whole and healthy?**

❑ **What would this tell us about you?**

Giving Encouragement and Challenge
Read 2 Kings 2:1-5 and discuss the following questions:

❑ **God sent Elijah on a thirty-plus mile trip, on foot, to visit two schools of prophets. Why would He do this?**
(Even these young prophets knew this was Elijah's last day. But there is more to God's design than simple farewell speeches. The schools of prophets were made up of young men who had left their homes and families to be trained in the prophetic ministry. They had sacrificed their careers for the sake of God's calling to proclaim God's Word to a dark and broken world. Who better than Elijah to give them encouragement and challenge? Elijah knew more than anyone the rigors of the life to which they were called. He knew more than anyone the magnitude of the task to which they were committed. They needed encouragement and challenge to persevere. Who better than Elijah to bring these words at such a significant time?)

❑ **What kinds of things could Elijah say to these young men?** (There are no right or wrong answers. Let the group respond according to how they have understood Elijah's life and ministry.)

Discuss the kind of person it takes to intentionally seek to build up and encourage others in God's work.

Lead the group through the Opportunity Analysis in the book. Help them see the opportunities before them to encourage and affirm others who are doing God's work.

Release the Power of the Spirit
Read 2 Kings 2:6-10 and ask: **What did Elisha request from Elijah? Why did he request this particular thing?**

140

(Elisha's request was not as presumptuous as it sounds. Elisha had seen God's power revealed in Elijah's life and ministry. It was no doubt overwhelming. Hence, Elisha was not asking to be bigger and better. He was asking for what he knew he would need to fill Elijah's shoes. Elisha's words when he parted the Jordan River in verse 14 illustrate this.)

Lead the group through the word choice exercise in the book. Invite group members to share the words they chose, and tell why. Discuss if there are ways you can each be more like Elijah on this point.

Carried by the Power and Presence of God
Read 2 Kings 2:11-14 and ask the group to project themselves into the situation. Here, as before, there are no right or wrong answers. Allow your group members the luxury of open reflection about Elijah's life, what he might choose to say, and what Elisha might wish to ask.

As you list examples of how Elijah was led by God, remember that, for all of Elijah's natural ability and strength, it was God who carried him throughout his life. He did not do what he did by his own devices and resources. His departure was simply a continuation of the way he walked with God throughout his life.

Lead the group through the Commitment I.Q. Test in the book. Have them share and discuss the reasons for their answers.

Pocket Principle

2 Make it a top priority to release the untapped potentialities within each group member. Let your group become a place where mutual affirmation can occur for each group member's uniqueness. Nurture an environment of mutual confirmation of the special abilities God has given to each of your small group members.

GROWING BY DOING   20–25 minutes

Removing the Blocks
Allow several minutes for group members to complete this exercise, then divide into discussion teams of three or four to discuss their responses.

When discussion teams are finished, call the group back together and ask: **What was the most important thing you learned from Elijah about being God's person for God's purposes?** Divide the group into prayer partners for a time of sharing. Close your session with a special prayer time. As the prayer covenants were to last for the duration of this study unit, allow prayer partners to spend time sharing and praying together. Challenge each set of partners to offer prayers of commitment and thanks for the opportunity to grow together as God's people for God's purposes.

Optional—Coat of Arms
Give each group member a large sheet of drawing paper and a marker. Instruct them to make a coat of arms:

❑ Draw a large shield on the sheet of paper.
❑ Divide the shield into thirds by drawing two horizontal lines across the shield.
❑ Draw a vertical line in the center section to divide it in half.
❑ In the top section, draw a picture representing one way you can effectively challenge and encourage someone in doing God's work.
❑ In the two spaces in the center section, write the first names of two people you can release to do God's work.
❑ In the bottom section, draw a picture representing one commitment you can make to let yourself be carried by the power and presence of God.
❑ Along the bottom of the shield, write a life motto for which you would like to be remembered.

GOING THE SECOND MILE   5 minutes

Challenge the group to spend some time during the next week defining specific ways they can nurture a life of style by completing the exercise in their books. Remind them that since their prayer partnerships were established for the duration of this study unit, each partnership will need to evaluate their desire to continue.

GROWING AS A LEADER

Now that you have completed your study unit, take time to evaluate your small group experience. Present these questions to your small group. Lead them in an open discussion, allowing them to express how they feel about their small group experience.

❏ Did your small group experience satisfy the personal needs of group members?
❏ Was there an atmosphere of acceptance, security, and trust among group members?
❏ Was this group experience something each group member valued highly?
❏ Do group members feel this group experience helped them get closer to God?